Tiny
Prisoners

Also by Maggie Hartley

The Little Ghost Girl

Tiny Prisoners

Two siblings trapped in a world of abuse.
One woman determined to free them.

MAGGIE HARTLEY

This edition first published in Great Britain in 2016
by Orion
an imprint of the Orion Publishing Group Ltd
Carmelite House
50 Victoria Embankment
London EC4Y 0DZ
An Hachette UK Company

10

A CIP catalogue record for this book
is available from the British Library.

ISBN: 978 1 4091 6535 4

Typeset by Born Group
Printed and bound by Clays Ltd, Elcograf S.p.A.

www.orionbooks.co.uk

Dedication

This book is dedicated to Elliot and Evie and all the children who have passed through my home. It's been a privilege to have cared for you and to be able to share your stories. And to the children who live with me now. Thank you for your determination, strength and joy and for sharing your lives with me.

Contents

A Message from Maggie

I wanted to write this book to give people an honest account about what it's like to be a foster carer. To talk about some of the challenges I face on a day-to-day basis and some of the children I've helped.

My main concern throughout all this is to protect the children that have been in my care. For this reason all names and identifying details have been changed, including my own, and no locations have been included. But I can assure you that all my stories are based on real-life cases told from my own experiences.

Being a foster carer is a privilege and I couldn't imagine doing anything else. My house is never quiet but I wouldn't have it any other way. I hope perhaps my stories inspire other people to consider fostering as new carers are always desperately needed.

Maggie Hartley

Prologue

She'd just put the telly on and had settled down with a cuppa and a cigarette to watch *Loose Women* when there was a faint knock at the door. She tutted, got up and peeped through the spy hole.

A pale face and big, frightened blue eyes stared up at her. It was the little lad from next door.

That's strange, she thought, as she took the chain off and opened the door to him. What was he doing wandering around outside on his own? He couldn't have been more than three. His clothes were filthy and tatty, and she noticed he didn't have any shoes or socks on.

'What is it, sweetheart?' she asked, holding out her hand and leading him into the hallway.

'It's my mummy,' he told her. 'She won't wake up.'

He handed her an empty container of prescription tablets but something else had caught her eye. Leading all the way behind him up the path and now on her hall tiles was a trail of tiny bloody footprints. His feet were covered in blood.

She grabbed her keys and picked him up. God only knows where his baby sister was.

'Don't you worry, little one,' she told him. 'It's going to be OK.'

But as she ran round to next door following the trail of wet blood, she wasn't so sure that it was.

ONE

Departures and Arrivals

After I'd waved the social worker's car off down the driveway, I closed the front door and breathed a sigh of relief.

'Phew, I'm glad they've gone,' said my ten-year-old daughter Tess, echoing my thoughts exactly. 'They were really strange.'

We'd just said goodbye to two teenage girls aged fourteen and fifteen called Hannah and Hayley. They looked a bit like twins as they were so close in age. Both chubby, with bright red hair and thick glasses, they would stare at you with deadpan faces. It had been an emergency twenty-one-day placement as their previous foster carers couldn't cope with their bizarre behaviour and I'd agreed to take them in while Social Services looked for another long-term placement for them. As a foster carer for the past twenty years, I was used to dealing with 'stroppies', as I fondly nicknamed difficult teens – in fact I secretly relished the challenge. But even I had to admit it had been a tricky few weeks.

Their behaviour had been odd to say the least. They didn't say much to me but they would walk around the house talking to people who weren't there. There was a Miffy mobile hung up in their bedroom that I'd forgotten to take down after a baby I'd looked after had left, and the girls had told us that the mobile had been saying things to them. Social workers couldn't agree whether the girls had significant mental health problems or they were just making it all up to freak people out. Sadly I thought a lot of it had been put on to get attention. I think they hoped that if they behaved in such a strange way no one would want to look after them, and they'd be allowed to go back and live with their birth mother. Whatever the reason, I knew three weeks wasn't enough time to even begin to tackle their issues. It hadn't been easy having them in the house, especially after school and at weekends when all my other children were at home.

The girls had left by 10 a.m. but there was no time to sit down and put my feet up. As a busy foster carer, I knew from experience that as soon as one placement left sometimes it was only a matter of hours before there was another child, or children, waiting to take their place. So I got to work stripping the two single beds in the room where Hannah and Hayley had been and gave it a good clean. I'd helped them pack that morning and tidied up as I'd gone along, so thankfully it wasn't in too much of a state. I was lucky as for the past five years I'd lived in a roomy detached Victorian house that I called the Tardis. It didn't look that big from the outside but it had six bedrooms and was spread out over three floors. Cleaning it was a nightmare and it was permanently freezing cold, but all that space meant I had two spare bedrooms especially for foster children.

In my forties, I was a single mum to my six-year-old biological son Pete, then there was ten-year-old Tess and her nine-year-old sister Sam – I'd been fostering for fourteen years when they'd come to live with me, when they were three and four, and they had never left. I'd been granted permanency, which meant that it had been agreed at a Social Services panel that they would remain with me for ever. I was hoping to adopt them but none of us felt like there was any rush as I already looked upon them as my own children. They'd come to live with us when Pete was a year old and he couldn't remember a time without them. As far as he was concerned, they *were* his sisters.

I'd seen their photos in a well-known fostering magazine that I subscribed to, and had been intrigued by Sam's disabilities as well as falling in love with Tess's beautiful blonde curly hair, so I'd found out more about them. They'd come from a family of four children. Two of the children had died from cot death at just a few weeks old and Sam had been left with brain injuries after her birth parents had tried to smother her when she was a month old – something they'd tried to blame on Tess who was only thirteen months old at the time. Sam had been left with cerebral palsy global and development delay, which meant she would always have the mental age of a toddler and she was autistic and half blind. After that there had been questions about whether their siblings had actually died of cot death, but nothing could be proven.

Her disabilities didn't faze me and something inside me just told me I wanted to give these two children a home after everything they'd been through. Before they came to me they'd been moved fifteen times. They'd even been adopted but the couple had changed their mind after a few weeks and they'd been sent back. These poor kids had faced so much upheaval, trauma and rejection in their lives but I knew 100 per cent I wanted to foster them, and amazingly I had space as two children were about to leave me and go back to live with their birth parents. It was one of those things I like to think was meant to be, and now I couldn't imagine our family without them in it.

Even though she was only ten, Tess was a great help with other foster children and all three of my kids were very adaptable. I suppose it was all they'd ever known. They were used to going to school and coming home and finding two new children had come to live with us and luckily they'd never resented that or got jealous.

It was just after lunch and I was taking the sheets and duvet covers out of the washing machine when the phone rang.

'Hi, Maggie, it's Simon here.' Simon was my supervising social worker at the fostering agency that I worked for.

'That didn't take long.' I laughed. 'The girls only left this morning. What can I do for you?'

'I wanted to have a chat to you about another placement. Social Services have been on. We've had a referral for a two- and a three-year-old and I wondered if you were available?'

He explained that they were being removed from their parents under an emergency protection order (EPO) that afternoon from a council house on a notorious estate half an hour away. Generally social workers try and work with parents and get their permission for their children to come into care, which is known as a voluntary care order or section 20. But in urgent situations where they felt the children were at significant risk or harm they could remove them under an EPO.

'Yes, of course I'll take them,' I told him. 'The other kids will be delighted that it's littlies.'

I was excited. My last few placements had been teenagers so I was pleased at the idea of having some younger ones to stay. It meant we could all do things together that my children still liked to do, like arts and crafts, baking and puppet shows, and it was a lot easier if they all enjoyed similar activities. I also thought it would be nice for my kids to be the oldest ones for once, as I knew they'd been quite intimidated by Hannah and Hayley.

'What else can you tell me about them?' I asked.

'I'm sorry, Maggie, but all I know is that it's a two-year-old girl and her three-year-old brother.'

'No problem,' I said. 'I'll wait to hear from Social Services then.'

'Great,' Simon replied. 'They should be with you within the hour.'

As soon as I put the phone down, it was action stations. As I expected, the other children were ecstatic that we were going to have two little ones living with us for a while. Tess especially was pleased that there was a little girl.

Whenever I know a new placement is on the way, I always think very practically – it's all about duvets and toothbrushes for me. I always have a big pile of toothbrushes that I get when I see them on offer, and thankfully the room next to Hannah and Hayley's old bedroom was already set up for younger children. The walls were painted in a neutral cream colour and there were two wrought iron toddler beds that had little sides on them. I knew from experience that many of the kids who came to me had never had their own bed before and that can feel quite scary, so having the sides on made them feel more secure.

I'm a sucker for anything by Cath Kidston or Laura Ashley and I always wait for the sales when I stock up on duvet covers. I put a tractor one on one of the beds and one covered in little yellow ducks on the other. Each bed had a fleecy blanket on the end of it, a little cushion that I'd made and a soft toy. I think it's nice for children to have those little touches there when they arrive to make them feel at home.

When a child has settled in I always let them choose something for their room – that could be a duvet cover or their own towels or a picture for the wall. To me it's important that they've got their own stuff to give them some sense of ownership and control. Many children that go into the care system have never had anything to call their own so I make sure that we personalise their room. I love sewing to relax and I'm a dab hand with a needle so sometimes I'll make bunting with their name on or a special cushion.

When the phone rang again I pounced on it, expecting it to be Social Services. But it was my friend Anne who was also a foster carer. We'd got to know each other as we both worked for the same agency.

'I'm running round like a mad thing here,' she said. 'I've got a couple of children coming in this afternoon on an emergency protection order.'

'That's funny, me too,' I said.

In a bizarre coincidence, she told me that our other friend Vicky also had two foster children arriving that afternoon under an EPO.

'Ooh I've got to go, the doorbell's ringing and I think that's them,' she said.

'Keep me posted,' I told her.

'You too,' she said.

As a single carer, it was great to have a network of local friends that I could call on for help. Particularly fellow foster carers who knew the pressures and strains of the job and we could compare notes. Because of confidentiality issues, we could never talk about the specific backgrounds of children we were looking after even to each other, but we could ask for general advice.

As I rushed around making sure everything was tidy, I kept one eye on the clock. But nearly two hours passed and there was still no sign of the social workers with the children. Simon rang back at 4 p.m.

'Sorry, Maggie, I've just heard from Social Services and I gather there's a bit of a situation with the mum who has mental health issues. The police have been called so they haven't been able to move the kids yet.'

'OK,' I said, wondering what on earth these poor children were being subjected to. 'Keep in touch.'

All we could do was carry on as normal. At 5 p.m. I was getting the tea ready when Simon called again.

'As it's the end of the day the emergency duty team are now dealing with it, but they've reassured me they'll get the children to you as soon as they can.'

'OK,' I said.

'You've got my mobile number so ring me in case of any problems.'

That was one of the benefits of working for a fostering agency, there was always someone you could call 24/7 if you needed them.

We had dinner and I got the children bathed and ready for bed. As I shut the living room curtains, I glanced up and down the street but there was still no sign of any social workers. It was a rainy night and my heart went out to the little two- and three-year-olds. It was getting late now and toddlers that age should have been getting ready for bed.

Finally, just after 7 p.m., the doorbell rang. I went to answer it and the kids came running through from the kitchen. Two women who I assumed were social workers stood there. One was carrying a little girl, and a solemn-looking boy was stood cowering by the other one. They both looked utterly exhausted and they were whimpering like frightened little animals. They were taking deep, gulping breaths like children do when they've been crying for ages.

'Hello, Maggie, we're the duty social workers,' one of them said, showing me some ID.

'Come in,' I said, ushering them into the hallway.

'This is Evie and Elliot,' she said.

One of the social workers put Evie down on the floor and she clung on to her brother. They both stood there staring at me warily with big, frightened blue eyes. My gut reaction was to scoop them into my arms and give them a hug, but I knew that wasn't the right thing to do with emotionally damaged or neglected children. It probably would have scared them even more.

Instead, I crouched down on the floor so I could make eye contact with them.

'Hello, I'm Maggie,' I told them gently. 'And this is Tess, Pete and Sam.'

They didn't say a word and I could tell they were shell-shocked. They were both absolutely filthy and I could smell them – an overpowering mix of stale urine and general dirt. Their clothes were grubby and I could see the head lice in their light brown hair. There were so many on Evie's head I could see her hair moving as they marched across her scalp like ants.

'Come on in and I'll get you a drink,' I told them.

Neither of them said a word or showed any reaction. Then Evie saw Tess and immediately held her arms out to her. Tess picked her up and gave her a cuddle, which was lovely, but all I could think about were the nits as I knew they'd be hell to get out of Tess's lovely ringlets!

Elliot stood there stiffly. He was so pale his skin was almost translucent and his eyes were red raw from crying. You didn't need to be an expert to see instantly that this pair were malnourished and underweight. Instead of the chubby cheeks and round faces that most toddlers have, they had a sunken hollowness to their faces and you could see every tendon in their necks. There were dark shadows under their eyes and their pupils were dull with no expression behind them.

The other kids went through to the kitchen while I had a quiet word with the social workers. Evie put her arms up to Tess and she carried her through, and Elliot followed them hesitantly. The social workers were both in their forties and looked like a strange pair, as one was in a smart business suit and the other one was in jeans.

'Do you have any information about the children?' I asked them.

'I'm afraid not,' one of them answered.

They explained they were emergency duty social workers and they didn't know anything about these children or their family. I felt so sad for these poor kids surrounded by strangers.

'I'm afraid there was a situation with their biological mother,' one of them told me. 'She'd escaped from a psychiatric unit and turned up with a knife and threatened to kill her own sister who had been looking after the children.'

She explained the police had been called and officers had spent hours talking her down before she'd been taken back to hospital. The children had witnessed it all.

'They were hysterical,' she said. 'The screaming was horrendous. It took a good couple of hours to get them out of the house and into the car.'

'They were obviously scared out of their wits,' I said.

It wasn't surprising really. The duty social workers both looked frazzled and couldn't wait to leave.

'Well, we'll be off then,' said one of them. 'One of our colleagues will be in touch but here's a mobile number if you need us.'

'Thanks,' I said.

As usual I was thrown straight in at the deep end not knowing anything about these kids or their background. Sometimes being a foster carer was a bit like doing a jigsaw puzzle. It was my job to pick up clues and put pieces of information together in order to get the full picture. What I did know was that these kids looked very bewildered and scared and I had so many other questions. *What on earth has happened to them that things have come to this? What sort of life have they come from?*

TWO

Nothing to their Name

After we'd said goodbye to the social workers I knew the first priority was to get these kids a drink and something to eat. When I walked into the kitchen, Evie was still clinging on like a limpet to Tess and Elliot was standing there looking terrified. The way he was hunched over reminded me of a little old man. He was very rigid and stiff and didn't seem to want to be touched, whereas Evie was the opposite and wouldn't let Tess put her down. Neither of them had said a single word since they'd arrived.

'Let's get you a drink then I'll sort out something to eat,' I told them gently. 'You must be starving.'

I sat them around the table on the little Ikea chairs that we had. They were special ones that had longer legs so little ones could reach the table easily but they were more grown up than a highchair.

They both looked at me warily with their frightened, glazed eyes, not saying a word or showing any reaction. *The poor things must be so confused and shell-shocked.* They hadn't got a clue who the social workers were or who we were.

'Kids, can you get Evie and Elliot some plates out please?' I asked Tess and Pete.

They got to work getting some plastic plates out of the cupboard and two little plastic beakers that I filled with milk. It's always a benefit having other kids in the house when new children arrive as it helps them settle. It shows them that this is a happy, friendly place that children like, so it puts them at ease. Evie especially certainly seemed to get comfort from Tess and she insisted on sitting on her knee.

I knew that asking lots of questions or bombarding them with information wasn't the right thing to do for these traumatised little ones. All I could do tonight was meet their basic needs – feed them, get them clean and try and get them to sleep. We'd worry about the rest in the morning.

I quickly heated up some tinned spaghetti in a pan and did them some toast which I cut up in little soldiers. As soon as I put it in front of them, they tucked in. Evie handed the spoon to Tess so she could feed her and she couldn't get it into her mouth quick enough. Elliot gulped his down too and within minutes both plates were cleared. The poor things couldn't have eaten for hours as they were absolutely starving.

'Well you two were very hungry,' I said gently. 'I think I'd better get you some more toast.'

While they finished their tea, I took their things upstairs. All they'd come with was a small battered old suitcase which I took up to their room. As I opened it up, the first thing that hit me was the smell which made me gag. It was revolting – a mixture of smoke and just general dirt and filth. As I rummaged through the contents of the case, I was more and more puzzled. Inside was just a heap of tatty, grubby men's clothes including pants and socks. There were no children's clothes or belongings in there at all.

I must have got the wrong case, I told myself. This must have been left in the duty social worker's car and they've picked it up by mistake.

I rang the number they'd given me to check.

'No, that's the case that came with the kids,' she confirmed.

'And there was nothing else with them?' I asked.

'Nope,' she said. 'That's all they brought.'

I'd no idea who had packed it or why but it meant that Evie and Elliot had literally nothing, not even a clean pair of pants or a soft toy between them. All these poor kids had were the grubby clothes they were stood up in. It broke my heart.

I quickly rummaged through my cupboards. I always have spare pyjamas for most ages as I buy them in the sales, and I knew I had plenty of boys' clothes as I'd saved a lot of Pete's old things. But I had nothing that would fit Evie. Thankfully my support network came into its own again. My neighbour Mark had a three-year-old daughter Kelly so I hoped he might be able to help. I got back on the phone.

'I've had a new placement come in tonight and I'm desperately in need of some little girls clothes,' I told him.

'No problem, Maggie,' he said. 'Leave it with me.'

Within half an hour, he turned up at the door with three huge black bags full of beautiful clothes. There were pretty blouses and jumpers, gorgeous pinafores and flowery skirts. I loved little girls' clothes and I hoped Evie was going to like them.

'You're a lifesaver,' I said. 'They're perfect.'

I was really lucky that I had such great people around me that I could rely on to help out in a crisis. Being a single foster carer, I didn't have a husband or a partner who could nip out to pick up some emergency clothes. So having a network of supportive friends who I could call on for help in a crisis was essential, and I knew if Mark couldn't have helped then I could have tried Vicky or Anne. Between us we normally had most things or knew someone who did and were always happy to help each other out.

I zipped the tatty case back up and vowed to stick it in the garden shed later. Foster carers are supposed to keep everything that looked-after children come into care with, because technically they don't belong to us, they belong to the biological parents. But I couldn't bear having that dirty old thing in the house.

By the time Mark had been round and the children had finished eating, it was well after 8 p.m. I could see they were exhausted but there was no way I was putting them to bed without giving them a bath first.

'Come upstairs and I'll show you your new bedroom,' I said to them.

Evie put her arms up to be carried so I balanced her on my hip and held my hand out to Elliot. He didn't want to take it but he was happy to walk alongside me. They both just stared warily at me. Neither of them had said a single word.

'This is where you'll be sleeping,' I said, showing them the little Ikea beds, but again there was no reaction.

The other children were downstairs watching TV, as I wanted to keep everything as calm and quiet as possible after the long, traumatic day they'd had. I talked them through everything so there were no surprises and they knew exactly what was happening next.

'I'm going to run you a nice bubbly bath and get you undressed now,' I told them.

I gently peeled off their filthy clothes. They were tatty and worn and didn't seem to fit them properly. Elliot had on a pair of age two jogging bottoms and an old T-shirt, and he didn't have any shoes just a pair of dirty socks. Evie was wearing a pair of leggings and a disgusting purple jumper that was matted and covered in old food stains. She had a pair of plastic sandals on her feet but they were way too small for her. Social workers always advise foster carers not to throw away their clothes if possible as it helps children settle to have familiar things around them, but nothing they were wearing was worth keeping.

Neither of them kicked up a fuss as I undressed them which was a relief. They were both very scrawny and small for their age. Their ribs were sticking out, but because they'd just eaten they had little pot bellies and they looked like the starving children that you see in third world countries. They were wearing nappies which I didn't think was appropriate for a three-year-old like Elliot and poor Evie's was so saturated with urine it was hanging down to her knees.

'Let's get this wet nappy off you,' I said gently.

Her nappy clearly hadn't been changed very often as her poor bottom was red raw and she had painful red sores all over her skin. Elliot's skin was really dry with lots of scratches and scabs. His nails were all bitten and the skin around them was peeling and bloody, and I wondered whether he had been picking at himself.

'I'm going to put some lovely bubbles in your bath,' I said in a reassuring voice. 'I bet you like bubbles in the bath. Now I'm going to put some toys in so you've got something to play with. Which end are you going to get in? Shall I help you both in?'

Both children got in willingly but it was an incredibly quiet bath – completely different to the usual noisy, messy, chaotic bath times in our house. They just sat there in silence and didn't play with any of the toys.

Afterwards I put a nappy on Evie and a pull-up on Elliot and helped them into clean pyjamas. *We'll tackle the nits and teeth brushing tomorrow*, I thought, as I could see how shattered they were. But even just a warm bath had done wonders. When Elliot had first arrived I thought he had brown hair but now he'd had a good wash I could see it must have been dirt as his hair was actually blond.

'Right, I think it's time for bed now,' I said.

I wasn't worried about how they were going to settle because I knew they were traumatised and in shock and they just needed to sleep. Most children don't give you any hassle on the first night because it's still the honeymoon period and they don't know you and you don't know them. They got willingly into their beds and I tucked their duvets up around them. As a foster carer it's not deemed acceptable to sit on a child's bed. Perhaps a child has been sexually abused and it might bring back painful memories. I didn't know anything about these children's history and I didn't want to put them in a situation that they weren't comfortable with or add to their trauma and distress.

Every year I had to sign what's known as a 'safe care policy' with my agency which is a set of rules and recommendations for foster carers designed to keep us and the children we're looking after safe, and I always have to follow those strict guidelines.

I picked up the teddies on the end of Evie and Elliot's bed. 'Night night,' I said to the teddies and gave them a kiss.

'Would either of you two like a cuddle and kiss?' I asked, but neither of them responded so I left it as I don't like to force affection on to a child.

As I left the room I did the same thing that I always do with little ones from day one – there was a CD player in the corner and I put on some classical music. I always play the same Mozart CD and I've found it really does help settle kids. It creates calm and after a while children associate it with bedtime. They know that when the music comes on then it's time to go to sleep. There was also a little plug-in night light that I turned on.

'Night night,' I told them, 'Sleep tight and I'll see you in the morning. If you need me, come out of your bedroom and yell my name really really loudly and I'll come and find you.'

Afterwards I went downstairs and put my children to bed, making sure I looked in on Evie and Elliot every half-hour. The first time I checked they were both still awake but they were just lying there in silence. I felt so sorry for them – nothing was familiar to them. They were in a strange bedroom, in a strange house with strange people and different sounds and smells. The second time I checked on them, Elliot had climbed across into Evie's bed and they were fast asleep, curled up together like two little hamsters. My heart went out to this pair. In a few hours their whole world had changed. Even though I suspected it probably wasn't a very happy world, it was all that they'd ever known. And now they were clinging on to the only familiar thing they had left – each other.

THREE

All Hell Breaks Loose

While Evie and Elliot had seemed to settle fine, I loathed the first night with new children in the house because I never got a wink of sleep. I wasn't familiar with their noises so every little snort or squeak would send me scuttling to check that they were OK. These poor kids were in a strange place and I didn't want them to wake up and be even more scared than they already were so I was always listening out in case of any problems.

My bedroom was just down the corridor from them and I'd left the landing light on and their bedroom door open, but nevertheless I found it impossible to switch off. I checked on them every half-hour until midnight and every couple of hours after that. Thankfully they were both in a deep sleep but unfortunately the same couldn't be said for me.

As I lay there in the early hours of the morning, tossing and turning and wide awake, I thought about how I'd first got into fostering. I'd always worked with children and seemed to have a natural affinity with them, especially kids who were challenging. When I left school I'd got a job in a residential children's home; then I'd worked for Social Services as a family support assistant. After that I'd got job as a deputy matron at a residential boarding school for maladjusted boys. It was very intense and exhausting. I lived on site and was on duty 24/7 during term time but I enjoyed it. For some strange reason, I liked stroppy kids and they seemed to respond well to me. I admired their honesty and I found them really intriguing.

After four years I'd had enough and a number of colleagues asked me to look after their children so I ended up becoming a childminder. When the children I was looking after all reached school age, I fancied a new challenge and that's when I thought about fostering. I was only twenty-seven and single but that didn't seem to bother the social workers and I was approved to take three placements at a time.

Back then in the late 1980s, foster carers didn't really specialise in one particular age group and I was happy to take on a wide variety of placements. Over the years I'd had babies, teenagers, children on remand, kids who'd been trafficked, refugees, disabled kids, mums and babies. I just did what I could for them in the time that I had, whether that was as basic as giving them clean clothes and clean sheets and a safe place for a few nights or looking after them for years, preparing them for adoption or successfully reuniting them with their parents. Over the past twenty years I must have fostered over 300 children in total.

Every single case was different and I'd learnt something new from every child. I'd had placements that had literally come for an hour. Once a social worker asked me to pick up a child from the police station and look after him for a couple of weeks. By the time I'd driven him home and given him a drink of juice, I got a phone call saying could I bring him back as his mum was being released. Most of the time I didn't know at first how long a child would be with me, particularly when they'd been removed from their parents in a hurry like Evie and Elliot had. At this stage I didn't know a single thing about them but in a way I didn't mind. Of course I needed to know about anything major like a medical condition but the rest of it I liked to find out for myself.

All of that thinking must have done the trick because I finally nodded off around 5 a.m – only to be woken up just after 7 a.m. by an excited Sam, Pete and Tess dancing around outside Evie and Elliot's bedroom door.

'The little ones are still asleep,' said Tess. 'Can we wake them up?'

'No, you cannot,' I said, feeling absolutely shattered.

Much to my impatient children's disgust, we let them sleep and there wasn't a peep out of the pair of them until well after 8 a.m.

'Good morning,' I said cheerfully, breezing into the bedroom when I heard them stir. 'Would you like some breakfast?'

I knew it was important to remind them again who I was and where they were. They'd had such a traumatic day yesterday and children as young as they were often forgot and I didn't want them to be scared.

'Can you remember that I'm Maggie and you came to my house last night and you had tea? And then we went upstairs and I popped you in the bath and then you went to bed and slept all night.

'And can you remember that I've got a big girl called Tess and a little girl called Sam and a boy called Pete? Shall we all go downstairs now and have some nice breakfast?'

They were both still really groggy with sleep and Elliot looked puzzled as he watched me opening the curtains.

'What are them?' he said, blinking in the bright morning sun. Surprisingly he had quite a husky voice for such a small, frail child.

'They're curtains, lovey,' I told him. 'We close them at night to block out the light so it doesn't wake us up in the morning.'

But he still looked puzzled at the whole idea of curtains. That was my first clue that all had not been right at home for this pair. They clearly weren't used to everyday things that the rest of us take for granted, like beds, curtains and clean sheets. Elliot seemed so pleased and surprised that he hadn't woken up that morning with a wet bed because I'd put him in a pull-up, which made me suspect he'd come from a home where there were no clean sheets even if you wet the bed.

As we all trooped down for breakfast, neither Evie nor Elliot said much. They'd not asked where their mummy and daddy were or how long they were staying. They just sat there watching, their big blue eyes following my every move. There was a real wariness about them, especially Elliot. I could already tell that Evie was more warm and cuddly whereas Elliot had stiffness about him and gave off a vibe of 'don't come near me'.

'Time to get dressed and brush our teeth,' I told them after they'd finished their cornflakes and they followed me upstairs to the bathroom. I got them a new toothbrush each and smeared a pea-sized amount of fruity children's toothpaste on the end of each one. I put the tap on and turned to Elliot.

'Open wide,' I said but he just stared at me with a frightened look on his face, his mouth clamped tightly shut. Evie looked equally as terrified. Then suddenly it clicked. They didn't have a clue what I was doing.

'Do you know what this is?' I asked Elliot, pointing to the toothbrush, and he shook his head.

It broke my heart that no one had ever cared for them enough to even show them something as simple as brushing their teeth. The poor things couldn't understand why I was trying to force this strange bristly object into their mouths.

'Kids,' I shouted to the others. 'Come and show Evie and Elliot how we brush our teeth.

'We do this every morning and every night to keep our teeth nice and clean,' I explained.

We all stood there and brushed our teeth in the hope that it would reassure them that it was a normal thing to do, but neither of them looked particularly convinced. I dreaded to think what sort of state their teeth were in if they'd never ever brushed them, but I wasn't going to force the trauma of a dentist's appointment on them right away. They wouldn't let me anywhere near their mouths, so in the end I gave them the brushes to hold but all they did was suck on the bristles for a few seconds.

'Well done,' I told them. 'We'll have another go tonight.'

At least it was a start and not bad for two littlies who had never even seen a toothbrush before.

After that it was time to get them dressed, but when I tried to change Evie's nappy she clamped her legs together and started kicking.

'No, no, no!' she shouted as I tried to lay her down. I assumed that it was because her bottom was so sore and she associated nappy changes with hurt and pain.

'Maggie needs to get this wet nappy off you and I'll put some nice cream on that will make you better.'

But she still refused to lie down. In the end I got Tess to go and get a doll and pretend to change its nappy as well.

'Oh look, the dolly's having its nappy changed. Well done, dolly,' I said.

It seemed to do the trick and it distracted Evie long enough for me to whip her nappy off, put some cream on her sores and put on a new one.

It had been a while since I'd looked after a child who was in nappies and after I'd changed her, I realised I'd put the disposable on the wrong way round.

'Oh, aren't I silly?' I said. 'Look I've done your nappy all wrong. I'll have to do it again.'

'Silly cow,' said Evie matter-of-factly. I was stunned. Had I heard her correctly?

Then she pointed to Tess. 'Bitch do it,' she said.

I was absolutely taken aback and I could see that Tess was upset. I was shocked that a two-year-old was using this kind of language but I tried not to show it. I couldn't tell Evie off as I knew that at that age she wasn't doing it for effect and it wasn't said with aggression. She was purely repeating what she'd heard or perhaps been called herself at home. The only way to deal with it was to try and make light of it.

'What's my name?' I said to Evie who just smiled. 'My name's Maggie, isn't it, and that's Tess? And yes, Maggie is very silly for mixing your nappy up.'

But that wasn't all she'd picked up. Later that morning when I told her it was lunchtime she told me to 'f**k off'. It was heartbreakingly sad that these were some of the only words this toddler knew, but this was clearly just normal language for her and I knew the best way to deal with it was not to react. If you make a fuss then a child that age is more likely to carry on using that word because they see it gets a reaction, so it's better to ignore it. Also, I couldn't tell a child off for using what they'd seen as normal, everyday language in the home they'd come from.

After all that I decided it was time to tackle the nits. I have a complete hang-up about them and the moment anyone even says the word I start scratching. Over the years I've found the only thing that ever works is a nit comb and when a new one comes out I'm always first in the queue. I swear if I ever went on *Mastermind* my specialist subject would be on nit combs and lotions! I sat Evie and Elliot in front of *Peppa Pig* with a little bag of sweets each and got to work.

'Everyone has this done when they come and live here,' I told them to try and reassure them. 'Even Tess has it done.'

I've found the best thing that works is to put conditioner on dry hair and comb it through with the nit comb. If a child gets upset then a warm bath with a quick rinse helps. I was worried about how Evie and Elliot were going to react but thankfully they were both fine. I did my best not to flinch when I got some huge ones from Elliot's head and poor Evie's scalp was literally crawling. She had masses and masses and I knew we were going to have to do this every day for a while in order to get rid of them.

That afternoon the kids pottered around the house. Again it was a blessing having the three older ones, as Evie and Elliot were happy just sitting near me silently watching them play.

Simon my social worker phoned to check how things were going.

'They had a settled night,' I told him. 'They're still terribly quiet today but that's understandable after all the trauma of yesterday.'

'That's great,' he said. 'I'm sorry, Maggie, but I still don't have any more information about the kids' history but I'm sure their social worker will come and see you either today or early next week.'

'It's OK,' I said. 'You know I'm used to working with very little info.'

It was a Friday and knowing how stretched social workers usually were, I was certain it would be at least Monday before I'd get a visit from anyone. But I always knew I could ring my agency in case of any major problems.

As the kids played, I started to plan out the next few days in my head. One of the first priorities was to get Evie and Elliot some shoes, as Elliot didn't have any and Evie's were way too small. There was an out-of-town shopping centre about a five-minute drive from us that had a big Clarks store so I decided we'd make the trip later on today. My three loved going there and mooching around the shops and I often treated them to a McDonald's before we drove home.

I was just digging out some wellies from the hall cupboard for Elliot to wear when the front doorbell rang. It was followed by the most horrendous high-pitched screaming that I'd ever heard in my life. Instinctively I knew that it was Evie and Elliot. I bolted into the kitchen where they'd all been playing just in time to see the pair of them running into the conservatory that was at the back of the house.

'What on earth's happened?' I said to my kids. 'What have they done? Have they hurt themselves?'

They were such hysterical screams I was worried that they'd been seriously injured. Pete and Tess shrugged, looking confused.

'Nothing happened,' said Tess. 'They went like that when they heard the doorbell.'

As if on cue it rang again, and I could hear Evie and Elliot's blood-curdling screams ringing out.

'I'll get that and you go and see them and check they're OK,' I told Tess, as I knew I couldn't send a ten-year-old to answer the door.

It was the postman who looked a bit bemused when I grabbed the parcel out of his hands and closed the front door in his face. Once I'd dealt with that I ran through to the conservatory where I could still hear the hysterical screams.

'Where are they?' I asked Tess.

She pointed to the corner of the room. There was a tiny gap between the freezer and the wall and the pair of them had crawled into it and were huddled in the corner wailing. I'd never heard anything like it. Tess, Pete and Sam were just standing there looking shocked.

I crouched down on the floor and reached my arms out to Evie and Elliot.

'It's OK, you're safe,' I told them, although I wasn't sure they could even hear me over the racket they were making. 'It was just the doorbell. It was the postman and he's gone now so you can come out.'

But they wouldn't budge. They just kept screaming and screaming and I could see their frail bodies shaking with fear. I felt so helpless. All I could do was sit on the floor near them and keep reassuring them over and over again that they were safe. Over an hour later their screams eventually turned to gulping sobs and whimpers but I still couldn't coax them out. They'd worked themselves up into such a state they were hyperventilating.

'You're safe now,' I told them gently. 'Please come out of there.'

Evie shook her head and Elliot edged back even further into the corner. I was starting to panic.

'Come on out and I'll get you a drink,' I pleaded. 'It can't be very comfy in there.'

But neither of them budged.

'You try,' I said to Tess. 'Maybe Evie will come to you.'

'Come on, Evie,' said Tess. 'You've been in there ages.'

But she wouldn't budge.

'Please, Evie,' she said, holding her arms out. 'Come and give me a cuddle.'

Thankfully it did the trick and Evie leapt into her arms.

Once she'd moved aside, I managed to squeeze into the gap and pick up Elliot. I could feel his little body trembling as he clung on to me.

We took them into the living room and sat them down on the sofa. They were both still crying and whimpering. I knew they were in too much of a state to take in anything or answer questions about what was wrong. Sometimes I think we use too many words with young kids, particularly looked-after children – that is, children in the care system – so I thought the best thing to do was just sit it out. Tess and I sat next to them for reassurance until finally, nearly two hours later, they were calm again. Afterwards they were absolutely exhausted and, to be honest, I was as well. I went into the kitchen to get them a drink and a biscuit and make myself a cup of tea. I couldn't believe how they'd reacted when they'd heard the doorbell and I'd never experienced that sort of extreme behaviour with any other child before. They were genuinely terrified.

'Why did they do that, Maggie?' Tess asked me.

'It's just a guess, but I think they were probably frightened that someone was coming to take them away again,' I told her.

These were children who had just been through a stressful, traumatic situation. Their mum had been running around with a knife threatening to stab people and had had to be talked down by the police, and they'd witnessed it all. God only knows what they'd been through before that. It was no wonder they were constantly in a state of high alert waiting for the next emergency. My heart went out to them.

One thing I did know was that I couldn't risk that happening again so I wrote a big note to stick on the front door whenever we were at home.

Please don't ring the doorbell – just knock quietly.

After all that drama I knew the last thing the children needed was a trip to the shoe shop so I decided to save that for the next day. It would be a nice treat for everyone and a chance to take the children's minds off things. Little did I know what was to come.

FOUR

Shoe Shopping

Those first few days were about keeping everything consistent for Evie and Elliot. I suspected they'd probably never had that structure in their lives before and I think it helps children settle in better if they've got the safety and security of a routine. They know breakfast is going to happen when they wake up and then they get dressed, lunch is at 12, then tea's at 5 p.m., and then it's bath and bed.

The day after the disaster with the doorbell, I knew there was no avoiding it any longer. I had to take the children shoe shopping as we couldn't go out anywhere if they didn't have shoes. I made sure that I talked them through it in advance so there were no surprises.

'We're going to go to the shopping centre and get you some lovely new shoes,' I explained. 'Someone's going to measure your feet and they'll hold them and put them in a special machine and it will tell them exactly what size we need to buy.

'Then we can choose some shoes and you can decide what colour you'd like to have. Does that sound OK?'

They both looked very solemn but nodded their heads. I had a seven-seater people carrier and Evie and Elliot watched while my kids all piled in. But when it came to their turn it was a different matter. As I tried to strap them into their car seats they started to shout and lash out. Evie was the worst, kicking and screaming, but I was determined not to give up. I'd had problems with getting Sam into her car seat in the past so I'd been on an autism training course when I'd been taught a special technique to get resistant children into a car seat without hurting them. It always worked a treat and soon Evie and Elliot were strapped safely in. I could see they were scared of the car, perhaps because they were worried they were being taken somewhere else again. Thankfully after a few minutes the screaming and the crying died down although they still looked very anxious.

Hopefully they've settled down now, I thought.

It stayed nice and calm right up until the point we passed the local police station that was on the main road leading to the shopping centre. We were just driving past it when two police cars, their sirens blaring and lights flashing, screeched out of the station and I had to pull over to let them pass us. As soon as Evie heard the sirens, she went into meltdown. She started crying hysterically and screaming – the same high-pitched screaming that had happened yesterday after the doorbell rang.

'No, no!' she shouted. 'No blood. No, no!'

My kids just sat there, unsure what to do, and Elliot showed absolutely no reaction.

We were literally minutes away from the shopping centre so I decided the best way to handle it was to just carry on and deal with it when we got there.

'I know,' I said as loudly as I could over Evie's screaming. 'Let's sing a song.'

My kids looked at me like I'd gone mad.

'How about "Old McDonald had a Farm"?' I yelled.

I thought it would either calm Evie down or at least drown her screaming out a little bit. I started singing and soon my three joined in. By the time we pulled up into the car park Evie was quiet, but my head was ringing with all the noise. Her words 'no blood' had alarmed me, and all I could think was that the sirens had been some kind of trigger to an event that had happened to her in the past. I wasn't going to ask her about it now as I didn't want to upset her again and I needed her to be calm for shoe shopping.

'Well, here we are,' I said cheerfully.

The shopping centre was absolutely heaving and I could see the children stiffen as they got out of the car. Evie held out her arms to me so I picked her up and took Elliot's hand. As we walked through the crowds, I could feel him pulling back on my hand and I literally had to drag him along. By the time we got into the shop, Elliot was squeezing my hand tighter and tighter and Evie was clinging onto me like a limpet and refused to be put down. They both looked scared out of their wits.

'Look at all these lovely shoes,' I said in a calm, reassuring voice. 'Isn't this exciting?'

'I love getting new shoes,' said Tess.

But the children didn't look convinced. I took a ticket and soon it was their turn to get their feet measured.

'Elliot, you're a big boy so you can go first and show Evie how easy it is,' I said.

He leapt onto my knee as the shop assistant put his foot in the measurer.

'It's all right, son, I'm only measuring your foot.' He smiled. 'Don't worry, it's not going to hurt.'

I could feel the poor boy trembling with fear so I held him close. He just didn't get the concept of what was this man was doing to him. There was no joy at getting new shoes like there would be for most children. Again it was something completely unfamiliar that he'd never experienced in his life before and it was terrifying.

'Nearly done now,' I said reassuringly.

I chose a pair of navy blue shoes with Velcro straps and I helped him put them on because his little hands were shaking so much.

'Can you walk up and down for me, young man?' the shop assistant asked but Elliot just pressed himself into me and shook his head.

'Don't worry,' I said. 'Let's do Evie's now.'

I lifted her onto my knee and took her plastic sandals off but as the shop assistant came towards her with the measurer all hell broke loose. She started kicking and screaming.

'No, no, no!' she yelled, lashing out at the man who looked stunned.

As her hysterical screams rang out through the shop, everyone turned to stare. I could feel people looking at us wondering what all the fuss was about.

'I'm sorry for upsetting her,' he said. The poor man looked mortified.

'I do apologise,' I told him. 'I've never brought them shoe shopping before.'

I tried to calm her down but nothing seemed to work. The shop assistant even called a colleague over to help but not even the two of them could get anywhere near Evie's feet and she simply wouldn't stop screaming. As a desperate, last-ditch attempt, I took the measurer and tried to do it myself but it was an impossible task when she was wriggling about so much. I managed to get what I thought was a rough estimate of her size and quickly chose some pink and purple shoes. Thankfully Evie let me put them on her.

'She needs to walk in them so I can check the fit,' the assistant said.

'Don't worry, we'll just take them anyway,' I told him, desperate to get out of there as quickly as I could.

I'd naively assumed a shopping trip would be a nice thing to do but by the end of it I couldn't get back to the car quick enough.

'Are we not going to the toy shop or McDonald's?' Pete asked disappointedly.

'I don't think it's a good idea today, lovey,' I told him. 'We'll come back again another time.'

I was utterly frazzled and as I strapped Elliot and Evie into their car seats I could tell they were exhausted too. I was starting to wonder what I had taken on. In all my years of fostering I had never seen children so traumatised that they couldn't even go out on a trip to the shops. I guessed it was the crowds and the fact that none of it was familiar that had got them so distressed. They hadn't felt safe there and I could see the fear in their eyes.

My kids had been extremely tolerant of Evie and Elliot's behaviour and I knew they were disappointed not to have the shopping trip I'd promised them. So instead I went to the drive-through McDonald's to get a takeaway.

'Well done for getting your new shoes,' I told Elliot and Evie as we drove home.

Yes it had been a hellish experience for all of us but I had to try and be positive.

One thing I knew we needed to do quickly was to try and get them used to going in the car, as I didn't want them to have a meltdown every time we went out. Over the years I'd learnt that a good way of desensitising children to something they are scared of is to repeat the experience, but in a safe way. So I decided that every day, regardless, I was going to take Evie and Elliot out for a drive. Even if it was just a two-minute trip to the postbox at the end of the road or to the local shop to get a pint of milk, I was determined to make them feel safe in the car.

The next day after breakfast I got all of the children together.

'We've all got a very important job to do today,' I told them. 'We're going to clean the car.'

I gave them all a sponge and filled two buckets with hot, soapy water and we got to work. My kids were in their element, laughing and joking and flicking bubbles at each other, and normally young children love playing around with bubbly water, but Evie and Elliot were unsure. I showed them how to wash the paintwork down and reluctantly they helped out. I didn't want them to see the car as a scary thing and I hoped that seeing my children being happy and playful around the car would help.

'Come on,' I told them after lunch. 'We need to go and get some cheese from the shop.'

I didn't even mention the word car but I opened the doors and my kids happily jumped in. It was only a two-minute drive to the local shop but I was determined to conquer their fears. As expected Evie and Elliot started to kick off the minute I tried to get them in their car seats but this time I'd come armed with every distraction possible. I'd moved their car seats to the back of the car so their screaming wouldn't distract me as much when I was driving, but it also meant that Tess or Pete could sit in between them and reassure them during the journey. If things got really bad again I'd brought some little bags of chocolate buttons with me to bribe them with.

Eventually I managed to strap both of them into their car seats but they were still upset on the short drive to the shop. So on the way back I got out my trump card – the Mozart CD that I played at night when they were going to sleep. By now they associated that with being relaxed and peaceful and I was hoping listening to that in the car would help calm them down. Thankfully it seemed to help and although they looked anxious they were a lot calmer.

'Well that was quick, wasn't it?' I said cheerfully. 'I said we wouldn't be out for long.'

When any child is placed with me I have to keep a daily log of their behaviour, how they've reacted to certain situations or things they've said or done. So every night when the children were in bed I'd sit down at the computer, type out my notes and email it over to my agency.

At the beginning, when a placement first arrives, my notes tend to be very detailed as it's a way of building up a picture of a child and what issues we might need to work on. This went to my fostering agency and every week Simon would read it so he was aware of anything odd or worrying. Once a month we had what was called a supervision meeting where Simon and I would talk through any issues that had come up with the children I was looking after, and I always found it useful to get another person's perspective on it.

Every month I also had to fill in a report that would go to the agency about the children and their progress and what they'd achieved and enjoyed. Simon would add his own notes to that about when he'd seen the child or children and how he thought the placement was going.

That night I sat down and made notes about Evie and Elliot's first few days with me.

Elliot is very fearful of everyday situations like the doorbell ringing or going out to the shops. He doesn't seem to like public places where there's lots of people or noise and he's very anxious and withdrawn. Evie is terrified of emergency sirens and need lots of reassurance. She's scared about going in the car and it's a struggle getting her into her car seat.

It was almost as if they were terrified of the world around them and I wondered what they had seen or experienced in their short lives to leave them so fearful. I made a promise to myself to find out.

FIVE

Answers

First thing on Monday morning, when the children had been with me for four days, it was time for a placement meeting. This was where Simon and the children's social worker came to my house for a meeting about Evie and Elliot. It was the first time that I'd met their social worker and I was hoping that he or she might be able to tell me a little bit more about the children and their family background.

Simon arrived first, which I was pleased about as he was there as my advocate. We'd worked well together over the years and I always felt that he respected my opinion. He was a bit of an old hippy and he liked to wear brightly coloured linen grandad shirts, flowing scarves and brown leather sandals.

He put down what I jokingly referred to as his man bag – a green hessian army-style shoulder bag which he carried all his papers around in – and handed me a carton.

'What's this?' I asked.

'Just a few eggs from my chickens,' he said. 'I thought you might like them.'

That was typical Simon, and you couldn't help but warm to him and his quirky nature. He had two grown-up sons of his own and had a good understanding of children and their needs.

'Can I say hello to the children?' he asked.

'Of course,' I said. 'Come through to the kitchen.'

Simon already knew Sam, Tess and Pete so he had a chat with them.

'And you must be Evie and Elliot,' he said.

As expected they weren't happy about being introduced to a stranger. Evie leapt into Tess's arms and Elliot clung on to my legs and was shaking with fear. Simon knew not to push things with them.

'I'm just going to have a little chat with Maggie then I'll come back afterwards and have a cup of tea and see how you're all getting on,' he told them, but they wouldn't even look at him. We walked through to the living room to wait for the social worker.

'How's the placement going so far?' he asked. 'Have the children settled in OK?'

'Well it's certainly been a steep learning curve,' I said, explaining again about the screaming when the doorbell rang and their fear of the outside world. 'As you saw for yourself they're very withdrawn and scared, which I suppose is only natural after what they've been through.'

Saying that, I suddenly hoped that their social worker saw my notice on the front door asking not to ring the doorbell – otherwise I knew it would send Evie and Elliot spiralling into another meltdown and there wouldn't be much of a meeting.

Thankfully she had. Soon I heard a very faint knock and the sound of the front door opening. A woman with short blonde hair was hovering in the hallway.

'Hello, I'm Jenny, Evie and Elliot's social worker,' she said, holding out her hand in a businesslike manner.

'Nice to meet you,' I said. 'Do you want to see the kids? They're in the kitchen with my eldest three.'

'Don't worry,' she told me. 'Let's get on with things and I can say hello later.'

I already had the feeling that she was what I'd call a box-ticker – someone who did everything by the book but wasn't particularly warm and friendly. The complete opposite to Simon, who had insisted on seeing the children first.

I showed her into the living room while I went to check on the kids and make us all a cup of tea. Evie seemed calm sitting on Tess's lap and Elliot was watching the others play.

A large part of the placement meeting was about filling in a series of yellow forms that gave me permission to do certain things, like take the children for an eye test or to the dentist. As a foster carer you don't have the legal right to even do something as simple as get them a haircut without getting permission first. We also sorted out the kids' MOT, as I call it – all children coming into the care system have to have a medical and that needed to be arranged.

'Also, just to let you know, an interim care order was heard in court this morning and granted,' said Jenny. 'We thought it was best after what happened last week.'

The order meant that Evie and Elliot's mother couldn't just turn up at my house and remove the children from me like she had tried to do with their aunt. It meant that, from now on, all parental contact had to be organised via Social Services. I thought it was the right thing to do and I didn't want the children involved in another traumatic situation.

'The court agreed that it was a good idea to get contact with their mother started straight away,' said Jenny. 'So I'd like to set up a visit in a couple of days' time.'

Even when children like Evie and Elliot are taken into care under an emergency protection order, supervised contact with their biological parents is still encouraged if it's considered safe. Mainly because the primary aim is for kids to go back and live with their biological parents if at all possible.

Jenny explained that their mum, Sheena, had been sectioned under the mental health act and was being treated in the psychiatric wing of a local hospital.

'I thought it would be nice if you could buy a "get well soon" card on behalf of the children so they could bring it with them to contact and I'll pick up a bunch of flowers,' she said.

'I can do that,' I told her.

But to be honest, the idea of starting up contact so soon made my heart sink. I'd only just got the kids and was still in the throes of getting to know them, but I was worried about how seeing their mum at this early stage was going to unsettle them. I was also concerned that what little work we'd done over the past few days would be wasted and we'd be back to square one. I'd been trying my hardest to make these two traumatised children feel safe and secure. The last time they'd seen their mother she was waving a knife around threatening to stab people, and I suspected they'd be very fearful about seeing her. Neither of them had mentioned Mummy and I knew the trauma of seeing her at this point could send them into meltdown again. But I knew I couldn't object. It was something that had been agreed at court and this was a new placement and I had to be seen to be co-operating with the social workers.

'What about their biological father?' I asked. 'Where's he?'

'Their dad Dean is currently in prison for assaulting Sheena,' said Jenny. 'The kids haven't seen him for months. How about I tell you a little bit about Social Services involvement with the family?'

'Yes please, that would be helpful,' I said.

I listened as she explained that Sheena had been in her teens when she'd met Dean. They'd both had unsettled childhoods involving abuse and domestic violence, and Dean had been brought up in children's homes. The couple became known to Social Services when Sheena was pregnant with Elliot because the police had been called several times after Dean had been violent towards her.

'When Elliot was three months old he was taken into care,' explained Jenny. 'The police alerted Social Services and said neither parent was able to care for him as they were both drunk.'

He'd spent eight months with a foster carer and then been returned to his parents at eleven months old. Both he and Evie, when she was born, had remained on the Child Protection Register.

'Unfortunately the domestic violence carried on,' said Jenny. 'Dean headbutted Sheena one night and threatened her with a knife. Sheena hurt herself getting away and the police were called.'

'What about Evie and Elliot?' I asked. 'Did they see this?'

'I'm afraid they saw everything, and I believe Sheena was holding Evie in her arms when she was attacked.'

Poor little mites. It was no wonder that Evie was so terrified of emergency sirens. In her life so far she'd been lurching from one emergency situation to the next.

Jenny explained that following the knife incident Dean had been charged with GBH and ABH and sent to prison.

'Even though domestic violence was no longer an issue with Dean inside, Sheena struggled to cope,' Jenny told us.

Social workers had visited her at home and found that she was drinking heavily and had been self-harming. A few days later Elliot had gone round to a neighbour's house saying he couldn't wake his mummy up. His little feet were covered in blood. The neighbour rushed around to find Sheena collapsed in the front room. She'd been self-harming, hence the blood, and had taken an overdose of sleeping tablets. Again the police and ambulance had been called and the children had been placed in the care of an aunt who lived nearby.

'And of course you know about the incident last week,' said Jenny.

Sheena had climbed over a fence at the psychiatric hospital and turned up at her sister's house threatening to kill her, which was when it was deemed unsafe for the children to remain in the area and they had been brought to me.

Hearing all this, it was no wonder Elliot and Evie were so terrified. They must have been living in a permanent state of panic and fear, always on alert wondering what was going to happen next.

'There's also one other significant thing worth mentioning,' said Jenny. 'We don't think the children ever went out much, if at all.'

'What do you mean?' I asked.

She explained that no one had ever seen the children except for a neighbour, who only recalled seeing Elliot once. It seemed that they'd practically been prisoners in their own home.

'What did they do then if they didn't go out?' asked Simon.

'Unfortunately the children are too young to tell us but we suspect they were mainly left to their own devices as Sheena had often been drinking,' said Jenny.

It was no wonder then that the children were scared of going out. The sights and sounds of the real world must have been utterly terrifying to them, the walls at home gave them the security that they needed.

These poor kids had been through a lot. It was going to take a lot of time and patience to make them feel safe and secure. Elliot especially had faced a lot of upheaval in his life that he was old enough to remember.

As one of the reports Jenny had read out noted: 'He's a sad little boy who is withdrawn and anxious.'

Before Jenny left we discussed the arrangements for the contact visit in two days' time.

'We'd appreciate it, Maggie, if you could drop the children off at the hospital. I know the duty social workers had huge problems getting them into their car the other night and they're probably more comfortable with you,' she said.

'I'll meet you in the car park and then I'll take the children in to see Mum. We think that's best, as Sheena was very averse to the children going into care, and we're worried that if you're there it might antagonise her.'

'OK, that's understandable,' I said, although I suspected the children would go much more willingly and happily if I was with them.

After we'd wrapped up the meeting I took Jenny through to the kitchen to see Evie and Elliot. They didn't even register her presence but she didn't make any effort to really engage with them. Social workers I'd dealt with in the past had got down on the floor and played with kids for hours in a bid to win their trust, but there was an awkwardness in Jenny's attitude to the children.

Simon and I had a chat afterwards.

'I've got a lot of paperwork to do tomorrow so if you want to whizz to the shops or do anything on your own I'd be happy to come over and sit with Evie and Elliot,' he said.

I'd hardly left the house in the few days since they'd been with me and whenever we had it had caused a major trauma.

'I might just take you up on that,' I said, as I desperately needed a few things from the shop.

Simon came round the next day as arranged. Evie kept falling asleep mid-morning so I'd put her to bed for a nap around 11 a.m. Simon had said hello to Elliot and tried to engage with him but he just completely blanked him. We had a cup of tea then I decided to test the waters with Elliot.

'I'm just going to pop out to get some milk from the shop,' I told him.

He looked absolutely horrified.

'No!' he shouted.

'Elliot we need some milk and I'll only be five minutes,' I told him. 'Simon will be here and I promise I'll be quick, quick, quick.'

Sometimes repeating something reinforces the message to little ones. But Elliot was having none of it. He went ballistic, crying and screaming and holding on to my leg so I couldn't even move never mind go anywhere.

The noise must have woken up Evie because she suddenly appeared at the top of the stairs and started screaming. I knew then there was no way I was going anywhere.

I was cross with myself for even trying it, but the only good thing to come out of it was that Simon had seen for himself just how hysterical and distressed these children got. When he'd met them the day before they'd been quiet and withdrawn but now he'd witnessed their extreme anxiety. It meant that he could record it in his report, so it wasn't just coming from me.

Simon was very intuitive and he stepped back and let me handle the situation.

'It's all right, Elliot, I won't go out if you don't want me to,' I said, trying desperately to calm him down.

He refused to leave my side so we went upstairs to comfort Evie. She was only screaming because she'd heard Elliot's distress, so thankfully she soon calmed down. By the time we'd changed her nappy and gone back downstairs, Simon had popped out to the shop and got some milk.

'Look, Maggie, I've got your milk so that means you don't have to go out now,' he said.

I could see Elliot's relief when he heard him say that.

Their reaction made me even more apprehensive about the contact visit with their mother. There was no way I was going to mention it to Elliot and Evie just yet as it was still two days away. Kids that age don't have any concept of time and are only interested in what's happening here and now. I knew if I told them that they were going to see Mummy then they would only worry about it and it would become even more traumatic for them. If I didn't tell them about it until the day there was less time for them to get upset.

On Wednesday morning I sent Tess to the corner shop to buy a get well card for their mum. She came back with a nice simple one with some flowers on the front. Elliot and Evie were crayoning at the kitchen table when I casually showed them it.

'Look I've got a card for your mummy,' I told them. 'Shall we write in it and say let's get better soon?'

Neither of them showed any reaction and just carried on drawing. They didn't even look up. I wasn't going to force them to do it as I didn't want to cause them any more distress. I was starting to question what the contact visit and this card was all for. Was it really about the kids and their interests or was it more about making their mother feel better?

'OK, shall I write in it for you then?' I asked the children.

Again, there was no response or reaction. When children are uncomfortable with eye contact, like Elliot and Evie were, I would ask them to look at my nose when I spoke. It was something funny to distract them but it meant they would still look at my face and therefore hopefully take in what I was saying.

'Elliot, look at my nose and tell me which colour pen you'd use if you were writing on Mummy's card.'

'Green,' he said, getting back to his colouring.

I did the same with Evie and she chose pink. Then I put the pens in my left hand and did some childish-looking scribbles in the card. My logic was the kids knew what I was doing and they seemed OK with it and I didn't want their mum to be disappointed.

It wasn't until after lunch, right before we were due to leave, that I told them about the trip to the hospital.

'We're going to go in the car now as we've got to take the get well card to Mummy,' I calmly told them.

I'd prepared myself for crying and screaming but neither of them said a word. They just looked a bit bemused and unsure, and I'm not convinced they even understood what was happening.

The only thing Elliot asked was, 'Are you coming too, Maggie?'

'Yes, chick, I'm coming in the car,' I told him, being careful not to say that I wasn't coming into the actual building with them.

Surprisingly the pair of them were very amenable getting in the car and they were quiet on the drive to the hospital. As we pulled up into the car park, I could see Jenny the social worker standing there holding a tatty, wilting bunch of pink carnations that looked like they'd come from the nearest garage.

I think because they knew Jenny, and they'd seen her at my house, they got out of the car calmly and I strapped Evie into her buggy. She was tightly clutching on to the stuffed bunny that she'd taken from her bedroom at my house, its head nestled in the crook of her arm.

'Do you want to hold the flowers and give them to Mummy?' Jenny asked Elliot.

'No,' he said firmly.

He refused to take her hand and walked alongside the buggy instead.

I watched them walk across the car park to the front entrance of the psychiatric wing of the hospital, but halfway there Elliot suddenly stopped, turned around and ran back to me.

'No, lovey,' I said. 'You've got to go and give the card to Mummy.'

He looked so frightened, my heart went out to him.

I took him back over to Jenny and as they walked towards the hospital again his head was turned round and he was watching me the whole time. All I could do was give him a reassuring smile. As they got towards the entrance, Evie started melting down, and her high-pitched screams rang out across the car park.

They went inside and as I stood next to the car, I could see Elliot watching me through the glass doors. He looked so apprehensive and unsure. I could see Jenny was getting stressed trying to talk to the receptionist while crouching down to try and comfort Evie, who was thrashing around in the pushchair. Every time the sliding glass entrance doors opened, I could hear her screaming out, 'No, no, no!'

Soon the children disappeared out of sight and I waited by the car unsure about how long they'd be. I knew it wouldn't be a long visit but even I was surprised when they came walking out a few minutes later. They can't have been in there more than three minutes and all I could think was that Mum had come into reception and they'd handed her the card and flowers and then it was all over.

When Elliot came out he saw me and before Jenny could stop him, he came running across the car park towards the car. The door was open and he leapt into his car seat in the back.

'Home now,' he gasped.

He looked shell-shocked and I could tell he couldn't get away from there quick enough. Poor Evie was still screaming and her hair was all matted and wet with sweat. I got her out of the buggy and gave her a cuddle.

'It's OK, you can stop now,' I told her, holding her tight.

Just like that she was quiet. I felt her tense little body relax in my arms and she gave a huge sigh of exhaustion and relief.

'Well that went well,' said Jenny in a forced, overly cheerful voice. 'I'll be in touch.'

She drove off while I got the children into their car seats. They didn't put up any resistance and I knew they couldn't wait to get away from there. I'm not sure that either of them had really understood what had just happened. I didn't ask them anything about it. They'd been through enough today and I didn't want to cause them any more stress. I always prefer children to volunteer information about contact visits rather than me bombarding them with lots of questions.

I agree with social workers in that contact is important but it depends on the child and where they're at. Forcing Evie and Elliot to go and see their mum in a psychiatric hospital at that early stage was in my mind pointless and unnecessary. It was purely an exercise in box-ticking for the court and not actually about the children, and it was really frustrating for me having to be the one who put them through that.

As we pulled into the driveway, I could see how relieved they were to be back. They'd only been with me for seven days but already they viewed this as their safe place and felt secure within those four walls. And I knew that was where we were going to have a stay while I tried to get these children used to the outside world.

SIX

House Arrest

Sam finished her cereal, put down her spoon, and turned up the volume on the CD player. It was *Now That's What I Call Music Eighty-something* playing for what felt the millionth time but nobody minded.

The one thing Sam loved to do despite all her disabilities was to dance and Tess and Pete needed no encouragement. They all jumped up off their chairs and started boogieing to the music. It wasn't long before I was jigging around the kitchen in my bare feet and dressing gown and Pete was showing me his best break-dancing moves.

'I can do that!' said Tess, trying to spin on her head on the kitchen floor next to him.

I glanced over at Evie and Elliot who were sitting there silently watching us. They were looking at us all like we were mad as we danced around the kitchen in our pyjamas.

'We often have a little boogie after breakfast,' I told them. 'It makes us happy.'

I didn't want to pressure them into joining us but I could see that they were curious. Over those first few days and weeks I felt it was important for them to see people, especially other children, having fun. Unfortunately in the life they'd led they didn't know how to enjoy themselves. There was no joy or laughter in their little world and I hadn't seen either of them smile since they'd arrived. It was our job to try and teach them to relax and have fun and the best way to learn that was from seeing other people do it. It was also a good way of getting them used to loud sounds and smiling people.

By now I knew the children didn't cope well with going out in public so I'd accepted the fact that we were going to be under house arrest for the next few weeks, if not months. It was going to be a long summer holiday for me and my children but I knew it was important to try and make Evie and Elliot to feel as settled and as safe as they could.

Even though they'd been with us two weeks they were still very anxious and on edge. The sound of the doorbell ringing was enough to send them into a frenzy of fear and it would take hours to reassure them and calm them down.

Despite the fact I'd pinned a huge note to the door saying please don't ring it, I couldn't believe the number of people who still ignored it. That morning after breakfast the bin men and the postman rang the bell and I'd just managed to calm the kids down when it rang a third time. Evie and Elliot fled screaming and crying into the conservatory and we were back to square one again. I was absolutely livid. I marched to the front door where the poor milkman bore the brunt of my frustration. He looked at me like I was a crazy as I ripped the doorbell out of the wall, wires and all.

'Didn't you see my note?' I asked him.

'Sorry, love, I've just come for my milk money,' he said apologetically.

It may have been done in a fit of temper, but pulling the doorbell out was the best thing I ever did. 'Why didn't I do that the first day they arrived?' I said to Tess, cross with myself. 'It could have saved us so much bother.'

I left the note on the door and people were forced to knock, which thankfully didn't seem to bother the kids at all.

Unfortunately it wasn't just the doorbell that was the problem. Almost any other loud, unexpected noise sent the children into a screaming fit. Anything from Tess dropping a pan or the back door slamming in the wind, to the hum of the tumble dryer or our old petrol lawn mower revving up, would send them running for their hiding place in the tiny gap between the freezer and the wall. Huddled up there together in the corner was obviously where they felt safe. We'd always manage to coax Evie out first and then eventually Elliot would follow, both exhausted from sobbing.

As well as their fear of loud noises, the children were still very clingy. Evie was glued to my hip the majority of the time and Elliot would stand next to me like a stiff little soldier, as close as he could possibly get without actually touching me. They hated doors being closed and I couldn't even go to the loo on my own. It wouldn't have been appropriate to bring the children into the toilet with me and, to be honest, I didn't really want an audience when I was going for a wee. But if I shut the door they would sit outside crying.

So I came up with a plan. One morning when I went to the toilet, the children followed me as usual and sat outside on the landing.

'Maggie,' they whimpered. 'Maggie where are you?'

I hated hearing them getting upset so I took off the cardigan I was wearing and wedged it in the bathroom door. They couldn't see me but they could still hear my voice so I could talk to them constantly and reassure them.

'Shall we sing "Twinkle Twinkle"?' I yelled.

It did the trick and their whimpering and crying stopped instantly.

Thank goodness no one else is here to see this, I thought as I belted out nursery rhymes from inside the toilet.

There was one other surprising development in those first few weeks. I was in the kitchen one day when I heard Evie shouting something to me.

'What's she saying?' I asked Tess, as I was a little bit deaf in one ear.

'She's asking about when lunch is ready and she's calling you Mummy.'

'Mummy?' I asked, puzzled. 'Who's Mummy?'

'You!' said Tess. 'Evie is calling you Mummy.'

It felt bizarre because, in all my twenty years of fostering, not one single child had ever called me Mummy. Even Pete, my only biological child, called me Maggie. I think it was because there were no other adults in the house saying, 'Pass this to Mummy' or 'Go and show Mummy'. So he'd always just called me Maggie like Sam and Tess had and it had never bothered me. I knew I couldn't tell Evie to stop calling me Mummy as that would seem like I was rejecting her so I made a joke out of it.

'I'm not Mummy,' I said to Evie. 'What's my name?'

'Mummy,' she said.

'It's Maggie,' said Elliot.

'That's right, Elliot,' I said. 'I'm Maggie, aren't I?'

But from then on, Evie insisted on calling me Mummy. Fortunately the other children accepted it and didn't seem to mind. It felt very strange to me, though, and I made sure I mentioned it to Simon straight away as I suspected the children's social worker Jenny was probably going to have a fit about it.

'I've not asked her to do this but just to let you know that Evie has started to call me Mummy,' I told him.

He agreed with me that it wasn't right to tell her not to call me that.

'I think in a way it's progress,' he said. 'Your job as a foster carer is to get Evie to attach emotionally to you and her calling you Mummy means she's doing that, so in a way it's a positive thing.'

Even though it felt odd, it was understandable. Evie saw all these children in books and on TV programmes calling someone Mummy and I was doing all the things that these women did, like cuddling her, feeding her, changing her and nurturing her. It was based on her belief about what mummies were and I was fulfilling that role. I think it was also about control. So far Evie had had zilch control in her life and now she'd decided to call me Mummy and, as far as she was concerned, that was that and no one was going to stop her.

Something else we discovered about Evie was that she was terrified of blood. She'd always shouted about blood when she heard police or ambulance sirens but one afternoon Tess fell over in the garden and cut her knee. It was just a graze but it was bleeding a fair bit.

'Come inside and I'll put a plaster on it for you,' I told her.

When Evie saw the blood, she was very upset and concerned. She looked terrified and she wouldn't leave Tess's side.

'Tess hurt,' she said, watching her like a hawk. 'No blood, no blood.'

'Yes but she's all better now,' I reassured her.

'All better?' she kept asking Tess. 'All better now? No blood.'

I could see the sight of blood made her incredibly anxious and stressed and she needed a lot of reassurance. I sat her on my knee and gave her a cuddle.

'Daddy hit Mummy,' she told me matter-of-factly. 'Mummy bleeding.'

I already knew from the information that Jenny had shared with me at our meeting that Evie and Elliot had witnessed their dad hurting their mum numerous times. Again, all I could do was try and reassure her.

'Oh dear, that's not nice, is it?' I said. 'Did that make you feel frightened?'

Evie nodded.

The children seemed to live in a state of permanent anxiety and I was gradually trying to chip away at that. Even though I didn't take them out to any public places, I was still making sure we went for a drive in the car every day to stop them being scared of that. I knew they would have found going to a big supermarket terrifying but it was tricky as I'd got six mouths to feed and I still needed shopping. So instead I'd drive to the local garage that had a Co-op attached to it. There I knew I could park right outside and leave the older kids in the car with Evie and Elliot. The shop had big glass windows so I could always see the car and the children could see me while I ran up and down the aisles throwing stuff into my basket as quickly as I could.

I used the long days we spent at home to get them used to things that we take for granted but they didn't have a clue about, like clean clothes. At first they couldn't understand why I put their clothes in the washing basket every night.

'No,' said Elliot, when I put his T-shirt in the pile of washing. 'It's not dirty.'

'Yes, it is,' I told him showing him the stains all over it. 'It's got sauce from the beans you had at lunchtime on it so we need to wash it and make it nice and clean.'

They'd never seen a washing machine before so I showed them how we put the clothes and the powder in and then turned it on. They were absolutely mesmerised by it and spent ages just staring at it going round and round, like babies often do.

'Has it stopped yet?' I'd ask them. 'Can we get the clothes out now?'

Once they were used to clean clothes they went completely the other way. If they got the tiniest stain on them they'd ask for a new outfit and they wanted to get changed three or four times a day. It was all about striking a balance and I tried to explain that tiny marks didn't matter.

My other priority in those first few weeks was to try and build up the children's weight. It wasn't rocket science – I knew they just needed good, healthy food and regular mealtimes. But they were also very anxious about food, especially Elliot. Having regular mealtimes was obviously something new for them and it was clear that they'd often gone hungry in the past. There was almost a complete disbelief in the fact that three times a day there would be food on the table no matter what and Elliot was constantly checking that I had enough food to feed him.

'Is it lunchtime now?' he would ask as soon as we'd finished breakfast. 'Are we having lunch later?'

Neither of them could tell the time yet but they both knew when it was time to eat way before I even looked at the clock, and they would wolf everything down so quickly. The only food they seemed to recognise was tinned spaghetti hoops and toast but I knew that I had to introduce a broader range of flavours into their diet. They didn't know what fruit and vegetables were but they discovered they loved carrots and broccoli, which we all called 'trees', and they wouldn't eat any fruit except apples and bananas. My proudest moment was getting them to eat hummus which they loved, although the day I made fish pie you would have thought I was trying to kill them judging by their disgusted faces.

One night I'd fed Evie and Elliot earlier and, as a treat, I'd ordered an Indian takeaway for me and the other kids which I thought would be way too spicy for the little ones. But they were still awake when it arrived and when they saw us tucking in they were both desperate to have some.

'Here, have a little bit,' I said, offering a tiny mouthful of curry to Evie.

I was worried that it would be too hot but to my surprise the pair of them loved it.

'More more,' said Evie, gulping down mouthfuls of chicken jalfrezi.

'Mmm,' sighed Elliot and he couldn't get enough of it. 'Mummy's food came to the door.'

I realised then that takeaways were something they'd had before at home and were familiar with them. We discovered they loved everything from Chinese to Indian and fish and chips.

The children had absolutely no concept of cooking or making something from scratch. I showed them how to bake a cake one day and they couldn't understand it. They knew what a cake was, but Elliot just didn't get it as I showed them how to mix the butter, sugar and flour together.

'That's not a cake,' he said, completely puzzled. 'Where's the cake?'

'We're making it,' I told him. 'We have to get all the ingredients and mix them together.'

The look of amazement on their faces when I took it out of the oven was astounding. In fact Elliot thought it was magic.

'There's the cake,' I told him.

'How did you magic that so it looks like the shop?' he said.

They loved it when I squirted a few drops of blue food colouring into icing sugar so we had blue icing drizzled on the top.

Over the next few weeks I worked hard on establishing a routine for the children to try and give them the security they'd been lacking in their old lives. The only downside was that any deviation from that routine would send them both back into a frenzied state.

The children had been with me around four weeks when one day I noticed that my car had started to make a funny noise. My friend Anne's husband Bob was good with cars so he said he'd take a look at it for me. I got in the front passenger seat while he drove it around the block. I knew I couldn't leave Elliot and Evie so they came too and were in their seats in the back. As soon as they saw Bob driving and not me, they were hysterical.

'No, no, get out!' cried Elliot.

'Mummy's car!' screamed Evie. 'Mummy's car!'

It was a case of one step forward and two steps back, but I didn't let myself get frustrated. It was still early days and I knew once the children were settled a little further down the line I could work on them being more flexible and adaptable. Everything had to be documented to Simon and Jenny in my regular reports, and Simon and I would talk through any issues.

'I've spoken to Jenny at length about how Evie and Elliot have been since they were placed with you,' he told me. 'I mentioned how fearful and anxious they are, especially of new situations and people.

'She feels with the kind of behaviour they've shown that they're probably not going to be adoptable.'

I couldn't believe what I was hearing and to me that was just plain stupidity. I believed that for every child, no matter what their needs, somewhere there was a unique set of parents who were perfect for them.

'It's such early days. We don't even know whether adoption is going to be an option for them or not at this stage,' I told him. 'But to write these children off at age two and three is just ridiculous.'

We were only a few weeks into this and I felt that was very short-sighted of Jenny to even say something with such serious consequences as that. I was confident that once the children had worked through their fears, we were really going to start making progress. Or at least I hoped that was the case.

SEVEN

Play Time

One thing noticeable about Evie and Elliot compared to other children their age was that neither of them knew how to play. If I put toys in front of them they would just stare at them blankly and not have a clue what to do.

Evie seemed to have a vague idea and she would push dolls and soft toys around in a pram but there was no imagination or role play. She wouldn't talk to the doll, pick it up or try and change its nappy, so I tried to encourage that.

'Oh dear, the baby's crying. Shall we get her out and see if she'd like a bottle?' I asked her. 'Or maybe she needs her nappy changing?'

Evie just looked at me like I was mad. Even though she was older, Tess still liked to play with soft toys and dolls and Evie watched her as she pretended to change the nappy on a teddy bear and give it some food. I could see that she was a bit bemused and wondering why the heck Tess was talking to a cuddly toy, but she was fascinated and slowly she started to have a go herself.

With Elliot I knew it was going to take a lot more time as he was older. The only way children learn how to play is if someone shows them. Most of us don't realise how much babies take in in their first few months and years of life. They need interaction and intimacy and it plays such an enormous part in their development. It's the kind of thing most of us do with our children without even realising it, like blowing raspberries on a baby's tummy, playing peekaboo or showing them where their nose is. Most parents constantly talk to their little ones when they're changing their nappy or while they're taking them out in the pushchair and pointing out cars and cats. With Elliot it was clear there had been no intimacy or any interaction from his parents. He'd been fed and changed sporadically but I suspected the rest of the time he'd just been ignored. No one had ever shown him how to play or have fun, so heartbreakingly he didn't know.

All I could do was go right back to the beginning as if he were a baby and start with the most basic of toys. So one afternoon I got out a little wooden bench and hammer and sat down on the floor with Elliot and Evie. The only way they were going to learn was by watching me do it.

'This looks like fun,' I said, talking them through everything I did. 'You get the hammer and you hammer, hammer, hammer the pegs through the holes.

'Can you see the blue peg and the yellow one? Which one should I hammer first?

'I think I like the red one. I'll go for that one first. What do you think?'

I asked lots of open-ended questions in the hope that I'd get some response but both of them sat there, staring at me blankly.

I kept going, talking about what I was doing as I hammered all the pegs through the holes, but still the children didn't show any interest.

'Do you want to have a go?' I asked Elliot, but he shook his head.

It was almost as if they were scared of the toys.

I knew I had to keep trying so over the next few days I chose some toys from the playroom to scatter around the house. I put some Duplo in the kitchen and a shape sorter and some simple jigsaws in their bedroom but the children didn't go near them. I also roped in the rest of the kids to help. We had a big wooden doll's house in the living room so one morning I grabbed Tess and we started playing with it while Evie and Elliot watched. Again, I talked through everything as I did it and I asked Tess lots of questions.

'Where does the bath go, Tess?' I asked and she put it in the kitchen.

'No, don't be silly,' I said. 'We have a bath in the bathroom. We cook our dinner in the kitchen.

'Shall we find the children so they can go to sleep in their bedroom?'

It was also a good way for the kids to get an understanding about the order of the rooms in a house and what went on in each one. I found the doll's house was always a good settling tool and in the past foster kids had often acted out things that had happened in their previous homes using the house and the figures.

Although I could tell Evie and Elliot were interested in what Tess and I were doing, they still didn't join in with our play and preferred to watch. A few days later I tried again – this time with the help of Pete and some Playmobil pirates. We acted out a little scene with the figures, firing cannons and sailing on pirate ships. Again Evie and Elliot just watched, slightly bemused by the fact we were putting on funny voices.

There wasn't much laughter in those early days and, to be honest, it was exhausting and frustrating at times. I'd wake up in the morning and wonder if I was going to get through to these kids at all today. I learnt to celebrate the little achievements. Whether all they'd done that day was pass me a building block when I was showing them how to build a tower or push a square through a shape sorter, I was pleased that they'd achieved something.

Because of Sam we had lots of disability toys around the house that came in really useful as they were very simple to work. One of her all-time favourites was a little dog and if you lightly pressed the button on its head it would bark and if you pressed it a tiny bit harder, it would make the dog walk. I thought Evie and Elliot might like it so I showed them the dog and what it could do.

'Isn't it a lovely dog?' I said. 'What do you think its name is? Did you hear it bark? Look it can walk too.'

They watched me intently but again I got nothing back from them. Elliot just stared at me blankly and didn't seem interested in having a go himself. After playing with it on my own for fifteen minutes, I decided to try a different tack. I got up and went over to the kettle, leaving Elliot and Evie sitting on the floor with the toy dog.

I busied myself making a cup of tea, all the while keeping one eye on the kids at the other side of the room. They just sat there at first but after a while I saw Elliot hesitantly reach out for the dog. He gingerly pressed the button on its head and it started to woof. Seeing Elliot touching it had made Evie want to have a go so she pressed it too. By the time I'd made my cuppa and sat back down, they were both taking it in turns to press the buttons and make the dog work. It was a real breakthrough and I made sure I heaped praise on them.

'Well done, you two,' I said. 'You made it work. You're very clever, aren't you?'

That seemed to give Elliot the confidence to try a few more toys but he would never pick up a toy himself and start playing with it. He'd only play with things that I'd chosen first and shown them what to do with. Elliot seemed wary of the toys – whether that was the fear of not being able to work them or fear about what sort of noise they would make and whether he would like it or not, I wasn't sure.

I also needed to work on the children's fine motor skills as their dexterity and hand control wasn't as developed as it should have been for kids their age. So we filled the long days at home by doing very simple activities like blowing paint with straws, Play-Doh, finger-painting and potato stamps. My kids still loved doing this kind of thing so it was very relaxed and there was no pressure on Evie and Elliot to join in. They could just watch if they wanted to, but I found they took the lead from my children who always got them involved.

With these kind of activities I would set them up but then stand back and let them get on with it. If anyone knew how to show little ones how to play then it was other children, and it was better than me hovering over them. I think my kids also enjoyed being in charge as that didn't happen when there were older foster children in the house. Evie and Elliot would hold back at first as they didn't have a clue what to do, but Tess and Pete would encourage them to have a go. So when they were blowing paint with straws, Tess handed them a straw each and showed them how to do it.

'You do it like this.' She showed them. 'Go on, you try it.'

While my kids were grabbing all different colours and throwing straws across the table, Evie and Elliot were still quiet and hesitant. They always waited for Tess or Pete to give them a new straw or a different colour paint to try. It was like they always needed permission to play.

Books were something else that the children didn't get. We were avid readers in our house and my children loved books, but they didn't hold Elliot and Evie's interest. They had no concept of fantasy or imaginative play, so the idea of talking animals or flying carpets was just bizarre to them. Their imaginations had never been allowed to develop. No one had ever played pretend games with them, they'd never dressed up or done puppet shows and put on silly voices. Again, all I could do was go back to the beginning, so we started by looking through lots of baby board books. The ones they liked the most were filled with lots of pictures of babies with different expressions like happy baby, sad baby, surprised baby. It was a great way to teach Evie and Elliot about feelings and for them to be able to give how they were feeling a name.

Halfway through the summer holiday and after several weeks of being shut in together, I decided to do a little experiment to see if the children could cope with a trip to Sainsbury's. I knew that it would have to be a very quick shop and also we had to go there with an aim in mind. Evie and Elliot both loved *Peppa*

Pig and they'd seen some slippers on an advert on the TV that they were both taken with.

'We're going to go out this morning and get you some *Peppa Pig* slippers like the ones we saw on the telly,' I told them one day after breakfast.

I deliberately didn't even mention the supermarket as I knew that would make them anxious which could then lead to a screaming fit or a meltdown. The slippers were a good distraction – if they had something to take their minds off where they were then the fear would be lessened.

I kept talking about these slippers, all through the car journey and as we pulled up into the supermarket car park.

'What do you think they'll be like?' I asked. 'What colour will they be? Do you think they'll have fur on them?'

My heart was in my mouth as I lifted them both into a seat on the front of the trolley but thankfully they seemed fine. They were right next to each other and they could both see me at all times.

We went straight to the children's clothes section where thankfully they had the *Peppa Pig* slippers. Elliot and Evie were so taken with them they even let me quickly try them on them.

I was amazed it had gone so well. They seemed fine so I decided to take a chance and do a little bit of shopping while we were here. Going to the supermarket was part of my day-to-day life and if I could get the children used to that then it was good for them and it would make my life so much easier too.

I'd brought some little cards with me from a shopping list game that we had at home. They each had a picture on them of things you might get from the supermarket, like carrots, toilet roll and orange juice. Again it was a distraction to stop them from feeling frightened or anxious. I gave them a handful of cards each and started to walk up and down the aisles.

'Shall we get some fruit?' I said. 'Who's got a picture of an apple?'

'Me!' said Elliot.

'Here you go,' I said, handing him a bag of apples. 'You put them in the trolley.'

While we did a few items on the list, I got the other kids to run round the aisles and grab some other bits and pieces that we needed. By now my children were very protective of Evie and Elliot. They knew how scared they got sometimes so they were always near them, like little bodyguards, checking they were OK. But our first trip to the supermarket went remarkably smoothly and it felt like real progress to me. We'd done something that they'd probably never experienced before without any fear or screaming. It had been quick and thankfully the supermarket had been fairly quiet, but still it was a public place and they'd coped. I was proud of them as it was something that a couple of weeks ago I never would have even considered. It gave me a glimmer of hope that at last I was starting to reach these children.

EIGHT

The Forgotten Child

After a month it was time to have a meeting to decide on a more long-term plan for Elliot and Evie. This meeting is known as the first review and is normally held at Social Services or my agency offices and a child's biological parents are encouraged to attend.

'Obviously the children's father is still in prison so he's not going to be there,' Simon had filled me in a few days before. 'Their mother's been released from hospital now but unfortunately Social Services don't know where she is so they haven't been able to contact her.'

Consequently, as neither of Evie and Elliot's biological parents would be there, it was decided that we'd have the meeting at my house, which was a huge relief. It was much easier and less stressful for the children to be in the safety and security of familiar surroundings rather than have to leave them with someone else or take them to a strange office.

I normally dread first review meetings as the biological parents can often be very hostile towards me as a foster carer, but I was looking forward to this one as it would give me a rough idea of how long the children were going to be with me. At this point I didn't know if they'd still be here next week, never mind Christmas, so at least I'd know Social Services' long-term plans for the kids.

Simon was there, as well as the children's social worker, Jenny, and also her line manager – a woman called Christine. They all said hello to the children while I got everyone a cup of tea.

'So, Maggie, how have the children been?' Christine asked me when we'd all finally sat down.

'Well, I must admit it has been challenging but I really feel like we're starting to make progress,' I said.

I explained about the screaming and their high fear levels of certain things and situations.

'Well Dad is obviously in prison and for now Mum has disappeared off the radar,' said Jenny. 'Dad has asked to be assessed to see if he would be a suitable carer for the children when he's released.'

'And what are your thoughts about adoption?' asked Simon. 'I think at the same time as assessing Dad perhaps it might be a good idea to get the ball rolling with the adoption unit at the same time.'

I could see Jenny wrinkle her nose. I already knew her feelings on this.

'As you know, I have serious concerns about the adoptability of the children,' she said. 'They're still very traumatised and fearful.'

I couldn't hold my tongue any longer.

'They just need time,' I told her. 'It's still early days but they're already showing progress in their behaviour since they first came. I need a good six months with them at least so they can work through their fears. Please let's not rule out adoption yet.'

I felt angry that someone was already deciding that Evie and Elliot were not adoptable. I didn't think it was fair to condemn them to a life of long-term fostering and potentially being moved around the care system. They'd had so much upheaval in their lives already and they needed the safety and security of their own mummy and daddy. After everything they'd been through they deserved to have their own permanent family.

'I agree with Maggie,' said Simon. 'If their biological parents aren't deemed suitable to look after them then adoption is the best thing for Elliot and Evie and if we could possibly do it then we should.'

It was up to Christine to make the final decision.

'The changes are small but they're happening,' I told her. 'Day by day the children are becoming more secure and I'm sure that will improve over time.'

Christine glanced through her notes while she chewed the end of her pen thoughtfully. Simon gave me a sympathetic smile.

'Well,' she said eventually. 'I think that while we're assessing Dad about his suitability to look after the children on his release, we should also start sharing information with the adoption team. I think it's in the children's best interests to look at both options.'

It was a huge relief and what I thought was the right decision. Nothing was set in stone but it was unfair to write Evie and Elliot off at this early stage. I could see Jenny was a bit peeved that she'd been overruled.

'While everyone's here I'd also like to get permission to start looking at preschools for both children as I feel that they'd benefit from being with other children their own age,' I said.

It was still early days and not something either child could cope with now, but I was mindful of the fact Elliot was approaching school age. That would be a massive challenge for him and it would be much less of an upheaval if I could get him settled into a preschool first.

'That shouldn't be a problem,' said Christine. 'We also need to start prison visits with Dad. If he's going to be assessed we need to see him with the kids.'

'How do you feel about that, Maggie?' Simon asked me. 'Are you comfortable taking the children into prison?'

'I think so,' I told him. 'As you know, I've done remand work before. Neither Evie nor Elliot has talked much about Daddy but I can try and work on that a bit more.'

As far as I was concerned it was a good outcome to the meeting. While all these different things were going on it gave me more time to work with the kids. Both these options were going to take several months so I knew Evie and Elliot were with me for the foreseeable future. I was pleased about this as the whole family had really got attached to this pair and we'd begun to love them.

Afterwards Jenny stayed behind as she said she had some information that I might find useful.

'Before their mum Sheena was released from hospital I went up to see her and get a key to their house,' she told me. 'I wanted to go and pick up some bits for her and the children.'

'And?' I said. 'What was it like?'

'It looked more like a squat,' she told me. 'The whole place was filthy and stank of urine. There was no furniture and upstairs it was impossible to tell whose room was whose. There were no duvets or bedding, just dirty urine-soaked mattresses on the floor and piles of dirty clothes everywhere. They obviously had cats as there were faeces in most of the rooms.'

I could tell by the disgusted look on her face that she couldn't get out of there quick enough.

'Did you manage to take anything for the children?' I asked.

Jenny shook her head.

'Everything was so filthy, there was nothing salvageable,' she said. 'Besides, as far as I could see the children didn't have anything. There were no photographs or toys or any personal possessions. If you walked in off the street you'd have had no idea that children lived there.'

It was heartbreaking to hear but it didn't surprise me.

Jenny and I also had a chat about Elliot. Over the past few weeks I'd realised that every screaming episode, except for when Evie was upset about blood or sirens, had started with Elliot. He was the one who instigated it, it was his trauma and his fear and Evie just picked up on that and joined in.

'There were some more notes in an old file that I found,' she said. 'It seems Elliot was very much a forgotten, neglected little boy.'

From what Jenny had read, it was clear Sheena had not bonded with Elliot from the start. When he was a few weeks old she'd told her GP she was having negative thoughts about Elliot and wanted to harm him and she'd been taken into hospital.

'I think, to Sheena, Elliot was the enemy,' said Jenny. 'He was very much disregarded and deemed a difficult baby and therefore a difficult child.

'Mum just ignored him and when Evie came along she focused all of her attention on her.'

'Maybe to her he represented men and men beat her up and hurt her,' I said.

It was desperately sad but seemed to fit in with my experiences of the children so far. Evie was a cuddly child and you could tell that she'd spent her life being picked up. Elliot had obviously been told not to speak so he kept quiet most of the time. I knew both children had been mentally and physically neglected but I could see that their mum had had some attachment to Evie and so her neglect had taken on a very different form to Elliot's.

'Evie knows how to give and receive affection,' I said. 'In fact she positively craves it and wants to be carried around all the time on my hip or Tess's. She needs the security of being constantly held. Elliot, on the other hand, is a frozen little soul.'

It was awful that this lack of affection had already had a profound effect on this little boy. You could physically see it in the way he dealt with certain situations. Like that afternoon after the meeting was over, Elliot tripped in the garden and bumped his elbow. When most little ones fall over, they tend to want a cuddle or a kiss or for you to rub their knee or their head where they're hurt. It was a nasty fall and whereas most kids would have been howling the place down, Elliot didn't make a sound although I could tell he was in pain.

'That must have really hurt,' I said. 'Do you want me to rub it better?'

As I came towards him he obviously thought that I was going to hug him and his whole body tensed up and he shot away from me like he'd had an electric shock.

If any of the other children ever fell over or hurt themselves he would always watch intently while I kissed their hands or knees or gave them a hug. He would wait anxiously for them to say 'all better now' and then I could see the relief in his eyes. He could see how affection worked but he couldn't cope with receiving it himself.

I had soon learnt that touching with Elliot was a big no-no. One night we were all sitting on the settee watching *Britain's Got Talent*. Evie was nestled under one arm and, without thinking, I naturally put my other arm around Elliot like I would if Tess, Pete or Sam were next to me. He flinched almost as if he expected my touch to hurt him. He was obviously so uncomfortable, he perched right on the edge of the settee as far away from me as possible. I tried to make light of it and turn it into a joke as he always seemed to respond well to humour.

'Silly me, my arms weren't listening,' I said. 'Don't worry they're in my lap now so you can sit back again.'

Looking at Elliot was like looking at a blank canvas, there was nothing there. His eyes were dead and they didn't have any sparkle to them. He'd received so little attachment that he'd just shut down and retreated into himself. All I could do was take it at his pace, not force affection on him and wait for him to respond.

I wanted to try and get him used to being touched in a natural, relaxed way. Bath times provided the ideal opportunity for this. I got Evie out first and helped her into her pyjamas while Elliot played in the water. Then Tess took Evie back to her bedroom while I got Elliot out of the bath.

'Look, I've got a lovely warm, fluffy towel here for you,' I said.

He stepped out of the bath and I wrapped it round him and helped him dry himself. This gave me the opportunity to gently pat his legs, back and arms dry.

'Right, let's get you into bed,' I said, wrapping him back up in his towel, picking him up and carrying him back to his bedroom. He was all snuggled up and I could feel that his body was relaxed. I knew even something as insignificant as this would help build on positive contact.

'Your hair's a bit wet,' I told him when we got back to the bedroom. 'Shall I give you a blow-dry?'

Elliot loved the hair dryer and again it gave me the opportunity to get him used to touch, as I had to ruffle his head and hair while I dried it.

I wanted to get him used to basic affection like patting his head or putting my hand on his arm – simple things that you do in normal conversation with children without even realising it.

Baby songs were also good for getting Elliot used to physical contact. Evie loved to play 'Round and Round the Garden' and for weeks on end, Elliot just watched.

'Can I do it too?' he asked one day.

'Of course you can,' I said.

I was so pleased but I didn't want to make a big fuss about it, as that would have drawn attention to what he was doing and made him feel uncomfortable. It was striking that delicate balance between encouraging him to give and receive affection without frightening him off.

As the weeks passed we sang lots of baby songs that involved arm, feet and leg actions. Evie loved sitting on my knee and grabbing my hands and making them clap together.

'Help me, Elliot,' she said. 'Clap Mummy's hands.'

Eventually Elliot plucked up the courage to do it and I laughed as he sat on my knee, grabbed my hands and forced them together.

Despite everything he'd achieved, I knew it was going to be a long, hard road to try and get him to move on from the past. It was my mission to make him feel worthwhile and loved for the first time in his life. The sad fact was, he knew his biological mum didn't want him and he had no sense of self-worth. You could see his lack of self-esteem in his physical appearance and the way he hunched over and avoided all eye contact. He was distant and withdrawn.

You could also see it by the way he was when he played. Part of the reason he was so anxious around toys was that he didn't want people to see him playing. I think he was worried about being told off or being criticised and it made him feel ashamed. There was one thing, however, that he really loved. As a keen sewer, I had a big tin of buttons in the kitchen and Elliot liked to take the lid off and play with them. We sat at the table and did button pictures, putting the different colours together to make button rainbows. I think what he liked about it most was that, at the end, we tidied the buttons away so there was nothing left and there was no evidence of his play.

It was the same with paintings and drawings. We did some painting with potato stamps and afterwards when all the kids' pictures had dried, I stuck them on the kitchen wall.

'Come and look at your beautiful paintings,' I told them.

Evie was delighted when she saw my display but Elliot went into meltdown.

'No, no!' he screamed. 'Take mine down now! Take it down now, Maggie.'

'That would be a shame as it's such a lovely picture and it looks so nice next to Evie's,' I said.

But Elliot was adamant that he wanted it taking down and I didn't want to upset him as he seemed genuinely distressed.

'I want it to go in there,' he said, pointing to the cupboard.

After that he would never let me put any of his artwork up on the wall like the others, it was all shut away in the cupboard. Sadly, this told me all I needed to know about Elliot's self-esteem.

That night I logged the incident in my daily notes and sent an email to Simon about it. I wrote,

In a way I think this symbolises Elliot's own experiences of life. He's been put away in the cupboard in the way his birth mother dismissed and ignored him. Making me put his painting in the drawer was as if he was saying 'I'm not really here. I'm not worth it.'

His self-esteem was so low he didn't have the capacity to be proud of himself and that was achingly sad for this little three-year-old.

It became my mission to boost Elliot's confidence. I decided one nice thing to do would be to make him a special cushion for his bedroom so that he had something in his room that was all his own. So I chose some lovely bright blue and red fabric and cut the letters of his name out in felt.

'Elliot, why don't you come and help me make your special cushion?' I asked.

He sat there, fascinated, while I stitched the letters on the front to spell out his name.

'Pass me my buttons,' I said and he handed me his favourite button tin and chose the different-coloured buttons that he wanted and showed me where to stitch them.

'There you go,' I said, when I'd finished it. 'What do you think?'

He didn't say anything but that night, and every night afterwards, he insisted on going to bed with his new cushion and he squeezed it tight like it was a teddy bear. It obviously meant such a lot to him that it was something special just for him.

Again I clung on to the positives, these were all little things but they were a step in the right direction. All I could do was provide Elliot with safety, security and love and hope that gradually he would have some self-esteem and belief in his own abilities. But I knew it was going to be a long road ahead.

NINE

Contact

We were in the middle of having breakfast one morning when the phone rang.

'Maggie, it's Jenny.'

My heart instantly sank as I hoped she wasn't ringing with bad news.

'Good news,' she said. 'Evie and Elliot's mum has got back in touch with us again.

'Apparently she'd been staying with an uncle the past couple of weeks since she was released from hospital. So that means we can start up contact with the kids again.'

'Fine,' I said. 'When and where were you thinking?'

'Well I think it's best if we use one of the contact rooms here at Social Services,' she told me. 'We don't know how Sheena's going to be and at least if it's held here there will be security around.'

'That sounds sensible,' I said.

Because of the knife episode they felt it was the safest option. Social Services offices in the city centre had special rooms with an emergency button in them in case of any problems and there were security guards outside.

'Do you want me to come into the building with the children this time?' I asked. 'I think Evie and Elliot would be a lot calmer and a lot more willing if I took them in.'

'I just don't think it's a good idea given how unpredictable Mum is,' Jenny said. 'You can obviously bring them but I think it's better all round if you wait outside just to avoid any trouble.'

She seemed adamant about that and I knew I had to respect her decision.

Again, I didn't want the children to get anxious about seeing their biological mum so I didn't mention it until the actual day. My friend Wendy, who was also a foster carer, came round for lunch with Joe and Jamie, the two boys that she was fostering. She happened to be going to a contact session at the Social Services building at exactly the same time as us. There were security issues around Joe and Jamie, in that biological family members had tried to follow Wendy in the past from contact to find out where she lived. We'd agreed that she would come to my house first and then I'd drive us all there in my car that had blacked-out windows. Joe and Jamie were two boisterous, noisy little lads and Evie and Elliot were very wary of them as they charged around the house.

'We're going to see our mummy today,' Joe said as we were eating lunch.

That gave me the perfect opportunity to talk to Evie and Elliot about what was going to be happening.

'Yes, that's right,' I said, turning to Evie and Elliot. 'After lunch we're going to take Joe and Jamie to see their mum and also your mummy's going to be there too so we can pop in and see her.'

Neither of them showed any reaction; I think having the two boys there had provided a welcome distraction.

After lunch I got Evie and Elliot's contact book ready. It's something I liked to do for every child that I looked after. It was an exercise book I'd got from WHSmith with cute little animals and birds on the front. Sometimes parents turn up at contact with sweets or toys for their child but they themselves leave with absolutely nothing. While they can't take their children home I thought the least I could do was give them something from their kids, whether it was a little model they'd made or a drawing they'd done. I stuck some postcards Evie had scribbled on in the book and also a photograph of the children that I'd taken the day before.

Evie and Elliot had a good lunch today, I'd written. *They played at the house with some friends before they came to see you.*

I made sure I signed it from Maggie the foster carer so their mum knew who the information had come from. When writing in contact books I was always very careful about the kind of language I used. So I wouldn't have said the children had 'played at home with some friends', I called it 'the house' and I always referred to them as 'your daughter' or 'your son'. I had to remember that until the court said otherwise, this woman was still Evie and Elliot's mum and I had to respect that. I didn't want her to see me as a threat or cause conflict because I knew that ultimately it wouldn't be helpful for the children. The contact book was also useful to give parents something to talk about during the visit as they often struggle to know what to say, particularly when the children are little. So I thought Sheena could ask them what they'd had for lunch and who they'd been playing with.

After I'd got all the children into the car and we set off, I made sure I talked Evie and Elliot through what was going to happen so there were no surprises.

'When we get there, Jenny's going to come out to Maggie's car then she's going to take you in a building to see Mummy.'

I glanced in my driver's mirror to look at them in the back and gauge their reaction. Evie was sitting next to Joe and they were chattering away so she was preoccupied. Elliot, however, was curled up in his car seat in a little ball. I could physically see his fear and stress at the thought of having to see his mum.

'No!' he said adamantly. 'I'm not going. I don't like it. Are you coming in with us?'

I knew I couldn't lie to him.

'Jenny's going to be with you and I'm going to stay in the car park and wait for you.'

'No,' he repeated. 'I don't want to see Mummy. I hate her!'

I knew I had to go through with this but I felt like I was making his worst nightmare come true.

Because of the security issues surrounding Wendy's foster children, we were allowed to drive into the private car park at the rear of the building. It meant Wendy and the boys could go in the back door without being seen. I was busy getting Evie and Elliot out of the car when I saw Jenny. As soon as Evie noticed her walking across the car park towards us, she started wailing.

'It's OK, Evie,' I said. 'Would you like to go in the buggy?'

She nodded her head so I strapped her into the pushchair, which thankfully seemed to calm her down. Elliot meanwhile was quiet but he was glued to my side like a limpet.

'Come on, Elliot,' said Jenny in a singsong voice. 'Come in with me and let's go and see Mummy.'

Elliot shook his head and buried it in my legs.

'Don't worry, I'm going to be with you,' she said, trying to grab his hand.

Well that was it. Elliot started to scream the place down. He was terrified and Jenny being with him wasn't any consolation as they hadn't built up any relationship yet.

I'd already made it clear in meetings that I was willing to take the children to contact but I wasn't willing to physically force them to go in if they didn't want to. I didn't think it was productive for the child or the parent and it was unfair on everyone to drag a screaming, distressed child into a room with a mum or dad whom they hadn't seen for weeks or months.

I tried my best to reason with him.

'Elliot, lovey, I can't make you go in and see Mummy but I'll just be sitting here in the car and it's going to be really, really boring so I'm sure you don't want to do that.'

But there was no convincing him. He clung on to me, howling and screaming. Jenny tried to grab his hand but he gripped my legs even tighter.

'Can you help me please, Maggie?' she asked tersely.

It was a real dilemma. I needed to be seen as being helpful to her but I didn't want to cause Elliot any more distress.

'Elliot, you need to go with Jenny,' I said, gently trying to undo his fingers and peel him off my legs.

I even tried giving him my car keys to reassure him that he was coming back with me.

'Take my keys,' I said. 'I need these keys to start the car so as long as you've got them you know I'll be outside waiting for you.

'Please, Elliot.'

But nothing reassured him.

'No,' he screamed. 'I don't want to see Mummy. I hate her.'

As a last-ditch attempt, Jenny tried to wrench him off my legs and pick him up but he lashed out at her, kicking and punching. I think then she finally realised that she wasn't going to get anywhere as she couldn't actually pick up a screaming Elliot and push Evie in the buggy at the same time.

'Well, I'll just have to take Evie in then,' she said.

The moment she said that, Elliot stopped screaming but he still refused to let go of my leg. Remarkably, given all this chaos going on around her, Evie had managed to nod off in the pushchair.

'Oh, she's asleep,' said Jenny, obviously annoyed. 'Well, I'm going to have to take her in like that.'

As far as I was concerned it was the best-case scenario as it meant she wouldn't kick up a fuss like she would have done if she was awake. I handed Jenny the contact book and watched as she wheeled Evie in through the back door of the building.

Elliot was still glued to my leg, whimpering. I gently stroked his back to try and calm him down.

'Elliot, look,' I urged him. 'Jenny's gone now. They've gone through the door.'

When he looked around and realised that I was right, he calmed down instantly and I could see it was a massive relief for him. I couldn't tell him off for not going into contact but I knew this was something I had to log with Simon straight away. So, while Elliot looked through some books in the back of the car, I rang the agency on my mobile.

'Simon, I just wanted to let you know that Elliot refused to go into contact so only Evie's gone in to see Mum,' I told him. 'The poor lad was hysterical.'

'OK, thanks for telling me,' he said.

'Also I just want to flag up the fact that I've always said I'm happy to take the children to contact but, as you know, I'm not going to get involved in physically trying to move the children. I just wanted to make that clear.'

I was covering my own back so I knew that if Simon got a call later on that day from Jenny complaining that I hadn't been very helpful then at least he had my side of the story.

'Maggie, I know you'll have done the best you could in a difficult situation,' he said.

Half an hour later Jenny came out pushing Evie who was still fast asleep in the pushchair.

'How did it go?' I asked.

'Mum tried to wake her up but she wasn't having any of it,' said Jenny. 'Never mind, we'll try again next time.'

Apparently Evie had peeped one eye open, looked at Sheena and then gone straight back to sleep. The minute Evie was wheeled back to the car her eyes sprang open and I couldn't help but wonder whether subconsciously she'd gone into such a deep sleep to protect herself.

Jenny handed me back the contact book.

'Mum liked the postcards Evie had done for her,' she said. 'But she noticed there was none there from Elliot.'

'I'm afraid he didn't want to do any,' I told her.

I was pleased Sheena had seen the postcards and kept them and the photo. The saddest thing for me was when contact books came back with the photos and drawings still in them and they'd obviously not even been looked at.

I got both children back in the car. We still had to wait another twenty minutes for Wendy and the boys to come out of their contact session so we passed the time with a game of peekaboo using a fleecy blanket. Evie seemed fine but Elliot was very quiet.

'Did you see Mummy?' I asked Evie.

'No,' she said.

'Yes you did but you were fast asleep in your buggy,' I told her.

'I 'wake now,' she said.

Elliot didn't say a word until we got home later on that afternoon.

'I didn't like it today, Maggie,' he said.

'I know you didn't, but Jenny has to make sure that you see Mummy,' I told him. 'And you will have to go again.'

'I'm not going,' he said. 'I don't want to see Mummy.'

My suspicions earlier had been right. That night Simon rang to say that Jenny had been in touch with him complaining that I'd not been very helpful.

'I told her you'd done the best that you could in a difficult situation and that you always put the children first.'

'And what did she say to that?' I asked.

'She thinks perhaps that you're the issue, Maggie. That the children somehow are too attached to you so they don't want to see their mum.'

'Well I very much doubt that,' I said. 'I think Elliot genuinely doesn't want to go. He's terrified of seeing his mother and that's nothing to do with me being there or not.'

With every single child that I'd looked after over the years, I'd always done my best to encourage contact if the courts had requested it and I was never negative about their biological parents.

Social Services didn't think that, at the age of three, Elliot had the ability or the understanding to decide if he wanted to see his parents or not. But I believe that when a child shows so much distress and fear about seeing his biological parents, you have to take that into account and realise that that child's extreme behaviour is telling you something.

Taking Elliot to contact with his mother felt like I was taking him to the lion's den because I knew that's exactly how it felt to him. But it was something that social workers were determined to pursue so we were going to have to go through it all again the following week. Jenny seemed to think that next time it would be a lot easier. I, however, wasn't so sure.

The following week I prepared myself to tell the children about contact. Mum had to be at the contact centre half an hour before the children were due. They did it this way as often parents wouldn't turn up for contact visits so it meant there was time to call off the session and avoid the children turning up to find that their parents hadn't. It wasn't fair to put little ones through that kind of rejection. It was also one of the reasons that I didn't tell Evie and Elliot about contact until just before it actually happened.

I was just about to broach the idea with them when the phone rang. It was Jenny.

'I'm afraid Sheena's not turned up,' she said. 'I've been calling and calling her but there's no answer. So it's not going to happen today.'

'No problem,' I said.

To be honest, it was a massive relief for me. The next week Jenny decided that this time she was going to drive round to Sheena's house, pick her up and take her to the contact centre. It was the only way she could be certain that she was going to turn up.

But again, an hour before we were due to leave, she phoned me.

'The contact visit isn't going to happen today unfortunately,' she said.

'How come?' I asked. 'I thought you were going to collect Sheena.'

'I tried to,' she told me. 'But she's been drinking and I don't think it's advisable for her to see the kids in this state.'

It was exasperating. How long were Social Services going to continue to push for contact when the children were terrified and their mum clearly wasn't interested? Given everything I'd learnt about their upbringing, I think it's fair to say Sheena's commitment to her kids was clearly zilch, so how could they think it was in Evie and Elliot's best interests to keep seeing her? This had to stop before any more damage was done.

TEN

Small Steps

Chopping up the onions and the garlic, I added them to the sizzling pan and gave it a good stir.

'It's spaghetti bolognaise for dinner tonight,' I told the kids as I tipped in the minced beef.

Elliot's face suddenly lit up.

'My daddy made that!' he said excitedly. 'I liked it.'

'Did he?' I said. 'Well hopefully I'll be able to make it as nice as your daddy's.'

Elliot looked the most engaged that I'd ever seen him. As he talked about his dad, his body language was relaxed, his serious little face came alive and he even made fleeting eye contact with me. It was clear from the way he spoke about his father that he had no anxiety or fear about him like he did with his mum. Any tiny scrap of warmth or affection that he'd had in his life had obviously come from Daddy and I could tell that he really meant something to Elliot.

'So was that as nice as Daddy's spaghetti bolognaise?' I asked after we'd cleaned our plates.

Elliot shook his head and gave me a wry smile.

'Well, when we see him I'm going to have to ask him how he makes it so tasty,' I said.

'Did you like Daddy's food too, Evie?' I asked but she didn't respond.

She didn't seem to have any connection at all to Daddy and showed no interest in him whatsoever. I wasn't sure that she even remembered him as she'd only been a baby when he'd gone to prison.

We hadn't been able to see their dad yet as we were waiting for the visiting orders to come through from the prison. But in the meantime I'd got the prison address and I thought it would be nice if the children could send him something.

'Shall we paint some postcards and send them to your daddy?' I said one afternoon.

The kids were too young to even understand the concept of 'prison' and neither of them had ever asked where he was. I also had an ulterior motive for the postcards. They were going to be the reason for Evie and Elliot's very first walk. After nearly two months of virtual house arrest, I'd decided it was time to get the children used to going out in public. They were fine now with being in the car and they could cope with the odd quick trip to the supermarket but they weren't used to walking around outside. Over the summer holidays we hadn't been able to go to any parks or playgrounds or have days out like we normally would but I knew eventually the children needed to be comfortable with the sights and sounds of the real world. They seemed a lot more secure and settled with me so I thought it was a good time to try it. Tess, Pete and Sam were back at school now so I could keep everything quiet and calm.

I cut out some postcard-size pieces of white card and the children painted squiggles on the front of them. Then when they were dry I wrote on the back of each one.

Dear Daddy, we painted you a picture. Love from Elliot and Evie.

Elliot helped me laminate them in my special laminating machine that he loved.

'You can help me feed the paper into it if you're very careful,' I told him.

Annoyingly it wasn't working properly and the paper kept getting stuck.

'Oh no,' I said after my fourth unsuccessful attempt. 'This thing is driving me potty.'

Elliot must have thought I was upset about it because he reached over and gently stroked my hand.

'All better soon,' he said in a soothing voice.

It took me by surprise as it was rare for him to instigate physical contact. It was something that he'd heard me say to the other children and I was really touched. After that it became our little phrase and we'd often say to each other: 'All better soon.'

After the postcards were finished I knew it was time to bring up the idea of the walk.

'I bet Daddy can't wait to get these cards,' I said. 'So this afternoon we're going to go to the postbox down the road and post them to him.'

I knew we had to start small and the postbox was only 200 yards away from our house. It was a ten-minute trip there and back at the very most, but I had to remember that the children hadn't been out into the 'real world' and this was a big hurdle for them to overcome. I lived on a fairly busy road and I didn't know how they were going to cope with the noise of the traffic or strangers walking past us or even how they'd react if they saw a dog or a cat.

I took them upstairs to my bedroom that was at the front of the house and we peered out of the window.

'See that red thing in the distance?' I told them. 'That's the postbox where we're going to post Daddy's cards.'

'Are we going in the car?' Elliot asked.

'No, we're going to walk. Then once we've posted them we're going to come straight back home.'

Both he and Evie looked edgy about the idea of leaving the house without the security of the car but I was determined we were going to do it and hopefully without any tears or hysterical screaming. Fortunately the gods were on my side because after lunch the children were watching a programme on CBeebies that they liked called *Balamory*. It just so happened that in this particular episode one of the characters went to a postbox and posted a letter. I couldn't believe my luck.

'Wow,' I said. 'How on earth did *Balamory* know we're going to do that today as well?'

It couldn't have been better timing and I decided to strike while the iron was hot. After the programme had finished we went straight into the garden and I got Evie the plastic toy buggy she liked to push around and the little tin pram that Elliot loved. It was an old thing from the 1920s that I'd picked up from an antique shop years ago and he adored it. It was solid and heavy and I think pushing that made him feel protected. Evie chose a doll to put in her pushchair but Elliot decided he wanted a car instead which he tucked up carefully in his pram with a blanket.

'Now we're going to take the babies with us to the postbox,' I told them. 'But then we've got to come straight back as we need to take the babies home.'

I thought if I used the idea of the babies then it would help reassure them that we were coming back. My heart was in my mouth as we all nervously stepped out of the front door; I knew there were so many things that could go wrong. I really didn't know how this was going to go and I hoped and prayed that we didn't see any police cars or ambulances as that would send Evie straight into a meltdown. If they did both get scared and run, my worst nightmare was that they'd both bolt in different directions and I wouldn't know who to go after first.

Elliot already looked very hesitant and wary. I handed him the postcards and he put them carefully into his pram next to the car. The little plastic buggy that Evie was pushing had a habit of tipping over so I'd attached a dog lead to the handlebars and I was holding the other end. It looked a bit strange but I knew it would help keep it stable and it meant she couldn't just push it off at high speed.

The children seemed fine walking out of the house but it was when we left the safety of the drive and got onto the pavement that I could see the anxiety creeping into their faces. Elliot stiffened up and made sure he was close to me at all times. If I stopped, he stopped – he was like my shadow. Evie seemed fine but I had the opposite problem with her and had to stop her from charging ahead.

I thought the best way to stop the kids from feeling frightened or vulnerable was to create distraction after distraction. So I talked non-stop and kept up a running commentary throughout the whole walk. If any other adult had listened in they would have thought I was mad and completely over the top but I knew it was the only way.

'Oh look, I can see the postbox in the distance,' I said. 'What a beautiful autumn day. Look at all the leaves on the ground. Can you see the orange and the yellow ones? And there are some conkers on the ground too. Can you see their prickly shells? I think that's a squirrel there climbing up that tree. Look at his bushy tail.'

On and on I went, hardly daring to pause for breath. I showed them how much fun it was to kick the piles of leaves and we even stopped to take a photograph as I'd bought my camera with me.

'Then we'll have a lovely picture of your very first walk at Maggie's house,' I said.

I never asked little ones to smile when I was taking a photo as I liked to capture their genuine expressions. There was certainly no smiling from Evie and Elliot today and they both had solemn, cautious looks on their faces.

The walk to the postbox felt like the longest 200 yards of my life but as they pushed their prams down the street, I was so proud of them. It was such a big achievement for them and it felt like they had made huge progress.

'Now who wants to post the letters?' I said when we finally got to the postbox.

Evie shook her head but Elliot was keen. I lifted him up and he very carefully posted one card through the slot then he peered in trying to see where it had gone. Finally he pushed through the other one.

I showed them the white notice on the front and looked at my watch.

'It's three o'clock now and in two hours at five o'clock someone will come in a red van and empty all the letters and cards from the postbox. Then they all go to a big depot where they'll sort them out and send them to Daddy and he'll get them by tomorrow.'

We'd done the job in hand, now it was time to head back home. Thankfully Elliot seemed a lot less tense on the walk back. I saw the relief in his face as he spotted our house; it was like a little weight had lifted as he was reassured that we were going back. But it was Evie who started to get edgy now. It was just after 3 p.m. and coming up to school run time. There was a school near our house so the traffic on the road was much heavier and there were more people milling around.

'Babies home now,' she said anxiously. 'Babies home.'

'We're going home now, Evie,' I reassured her. 'Look you can see our front door.'

That seemed to reassure her and she practically ran towards the gate.

By the time we walked in the house the kids seemed fine, but I was absolutely exhausted.

'How did it go?' asked Pam our cleaner, who was there that day.

'Well we did it and that's the main thing,' I said, hardly believing it myself. 'It went as well as I'd hoped. I wouldn't say the kids enjoyed it but they did it without any screaming or meltdowns.'

Later that night when all the children were in bed, I printed out the pictures from my camera. I looked at the photo of them pushing their prams through the autumn leaves and I felt so proud of them. Every time a foster child arrived I started a photo album and put in pictures of all the things we'd done so they would have memories of their time with me. Since Evie and Elliot had been with me I'd taken photos of them in all the rooms around the house because we hadn't been anywhere or done much else. The next day they watched while I stuck the photo in their albums and on the page opposite I wrote:

Evie and Elliot's first walk. We went to the postbox to post a letter to Daddy.

'You did so well, you should be very proud of yourselves,' I told them.

Now they'd done that, I knew I had to keep it up and get them used to going outside. I devised a fifteen-minute walk that went round the back of our house, along a muddy path past some fields and a park. It was a quieter route this time away from the busy road and it looped round in a circle so we ended up back at the house. I knew we needed an activity for the walk to distract them so I came up with a game.

I got two jars that had wire handles, a clipboard and a whiteboard marker.

'Right, kids, we're going on a jar walk this morning,' I told them.

They both had a puzzled look on their faces as I handed them each a jar and showed them the clipboard on which I'd written a few simple things for them to find, like a leaf, a stone and a twig. Next to each one was a photo of the item.

'When we find something on my list you put it in your jar and then we can tick it off on the clipboard,' I said.

They both seemed quite excited about the challenge, if a little unsure.

'Pram,' wailed Elliot. 'I want to take my pram.'

But I didn't want the pram to become his security blanket and something that he couldn't leave the house without.

'Well, if you take the pram you can't have the jar and play the game,' I told him.

Fortunately that did the trick and he resigned himself to going out of the house without it.

It was a simple device but something the children grew to love. Every day we went out for a 'jar walk' and they enjoyed doing childish, fun things that they'd never done before, like splashing in puddles, collecting sticks and stomping in mud. It was a good way to teach them about the world. I was pretty sure no one had ever shown them a spider's web before or helped them pick a blackberry from a bush or find a conker or an acorn, so we spent ages just stopping to look at things, picking them up and talking about what they were.

Getting them used to the outside world opened up a whole new realm of possibilities. They were confident enough to go to the little park around the back of our house. It was always very quiet and there was never anyone there so they felt secure enough to go on swings and slides. Elliot loved the zip wire.

I was also able to start inviting people around again. I was used to having a house full as Vicky and Anne would often bring their foster children to visit, but that had mostly stopped when Evie and Elliot arrived – except for the time Wendy had come for lunch before our contact visits. One weekend I decided to invite Anne and her foster children for lunch and amazingly Evie and Elliot coped. They seemed nervous and they stayed close by me but there was no screaming. They were just happy watching the other kids play.

'They're a lot better than what I expected,' said Anne.

'Believe me even a week or so ago we wouldn't have been able to do this,' I said. 'They suddenly seem a lot more settled.'

I really felt like I'd turned a corner with this pair. All those weeks of spending time in the house, developing a routine and teaching them to play had been worth it. Things were definitely on the up.

ELEVEN

Visiting Daddy

In early October the visiting orders finally came through so I could take Evie and Elliot to see their dad. He was in an open prison a couple of hours' drive away from us. I didn't know how long it had been since the children had seen him but it had been well over a year since he was sent down.

That morning, as I got the kids dressed, I told them where we were going.

'Today we're going to get in the car and go and have some lunch, then we're going to go and see Daddy.'

Elliot's face broke into a wide smile.

'See Daddy?' he asked. 'My daddy?'

'Yes, yours and Evie's daddy,' I told him. 'Don't worry I'll be going with you.'

For once Elliot seemed really pleased about seeing one of his parents and it was obviously something he was looking forward to. It was a relief after all the stress and trauma that we'd had around the visits to see his mum.

'Can I wear my new wellies with the dogs on so I can show

my daddy?' he asked as I was getting him dressed. 'Daddy likes dogs.'

'Of course you can,' I said.

It was good to know that Elliot had positive memories about his dad, even if it was about a man who had been very violent and abusive to his mum. I had seen that his father was the one person in his life who had ever shown him any scrap of love or affection. As well as the spaghetti bolognaise, Elliot occasionally talked about how he made him eggy bread.

Evie didn't say a word but she didn't seem bothered about the visit either. She showed more of a reaction when I said I'd take some bread so we could feed the ducks on the way.

'Yay duckies!' She grinned.

I was taking the children to see their father on my own. Jenny had decided there was no point in her coming all that way, which was a relief to me. Their dad Dean had co-operated with Social Services up to now so it was felt that he would have no animosity towards me and there would be prison guards there all the time. Going into a prison wasn't something that bothered me as I'd taken foster children on contact visits there before.

I got Evie and Elliot settled in the car. I wasn't sure what we'd be allowed to take in with us so I hadn't brought anything for their dad, and as I was going in with them there was no need for a contact book.

'Here's your snack for the journey,' I said, handing them a drink of juice and a bag of chopped apple and grapes.

The children seemed fine – they were more worried about having enough bread for the ducks than they were about going to see their dad.

'Can I eat a bit to test it's OK?' asked Elliot.

'Go on then.' I smiled as he nibbled on the crusts.

We broke up the journey by stopping off at a quaint little village for lunch. I breathed a sigh of relief when I saw a pond in the centre of the village green with several ducks on it.

We got back in the car and an hour later we finally reached the prison gates. I pulled up at the booth at the front entrance. I was worried about how the children would cope with all these security measures but they were looking out of the window, seemingly oblivious to it all.

'Hello, I'm a foster carer bringing Dean Maguire's children for a contact visit with him.'

'Name and driver's licence please,' he said.

Once he'd seen my ID and checked who I was, he ticked me off a list and the barrier went up. We drove through it and up a steep hill.

'You'll see the building where we're going to visit Daddy in a minute,' I said to the children.

They seemed quite happy and relaxed in the back, looking out of the window at the lush countryside. I could see the prison at the top of the hill in front of us and rather than the imposing building you might expect it looked surprisingly nice. It was very peaceful and green and the prison building itself was single-storey and modern-looking. I pulled up into a gravel car park and a prison guard came out to meet us.

'Maggie Hartley? Follow me over here,' he said, gesturing to a little building in the prison grounds that looked a bit like a scout hut. 'Their dad Dean is already in there waiting for you.'

The visitors' centre was a separate building so we didn't even have to go into the main prison. As far as the children were concerned we could have been at a normal contact centre, there was nothing intimidating about it at all. I carried Evie and Elliot walked along next to me as we followed the guard down a narrow corridor and into a hall. A man who I assumed was their dad was sitting on a tatty blue plastic chair and there were two prison guards sitting on the opposite side of the room in uniform. They were the only people in there and it was very quiet.

'Look who's over there,' I whispered to Evie and Elliot.

'Daddy!' shouted Elliot, his face breaking into a wide smile. He let go of my hand and went running towards him. However, halfway there he noticed the security guards and stopped dead in his tracks. His face fell and he turned on his heels, running back to me to hold my hand tightly. He was obviously pleased to see his dad but unsure of these other strangers watching him. We walked over to Dean.

'Hi, I'm Maggie, the foster carer,' I said. 'Pleased to meet you.'

He gave me a weak smile.

'Hello, son,' he said, ruffling Elliot's hair. 'Hello, Evie.'

He was a thin, scrawny man and he looked older than I expected. His face was haggard and worn, and he was wearing a tatty grey sweatshirt and jeans. He had the same neglected, haunted look as Elliot and it made me feel like he needed nurturing and some feeding up.

There were some toy cars and building blocks on the floor and Elliot sat down on the carpet and started played with them. I sat on the floor next to him and Evie plonked herself firmly in my lap. Dean got up off his chair but before he could join us on the floor, he had to ask the guard's permission.

'All right, sir?' he asked one of them, pointing to the carpet.

The security guard nodded his head.

He sat down on the floor with us and started playing cars with Elliot.

'Look at this one, son,' he said. 'This is a good one.'

He sat close to Elliot and leaned over him as they played together. Elliot seemed quite happy and didn't flinch at the physical closeness as he normally would have. As he pushed the cars back and forth, he looked up occasionally to catch his dad's eye and smile at him, and I could see there was a bond between them.

'Your hair looks nice, son,' he said, ruffling it. 'And that's a pretty dress, Evie.'

Evie completely ignored him. He reached over to stroke her hair but she pushed herself back against my body as far away from him as possible. She wanted nothing to do with him and Dean obviously took the hint and moved his hands away. Evie had no attachment to him whatsoever and made no effort to interact with him.

These sort of contacts are always quite exhausting as you have to make conversation with a stranger, and now there was the added pressure of two security guards watching our every move.

'Are they being good?' Dad asked me. 'I hope they're not crying a lot.'

'No,' I said. 'They're being very good.'

I could feel Evie snuggling into me.

'Evie liked her cuddles when she was a baby,' he said wistfully.

He must have been talking quietly at this point because one of the guards came and sat nearer to us as he obviously had to make sure he could hear our conversation at all times for security reasons.

'Are the kids eating well?' he asked.

'Yes,' I said. 'Elliot talks about your spaghetti bolognaise and how much he liked it. He says it's much better than mine.'

Dean seemed pleased about this and we talked for ages about how he made it. I knew this was really important for him. He was locked up in prison and had no control or choices over his children but it must have felt good for him to know that he could make a better spag bol than me. That way he felt that little bit more powerful.

'Maggie, I need a pee,' said Elliot.

'I'll take him,' said his dad, going to get up but the security guard jumped up.

'No, Maguire, I'm afraid you have to stay here. We have to be able to see you at all times.'

'It's OK I'll take both of them,' I said.

Evie was still in nappies and she'd been changed recently but I knew there was no way she would stay there on her own without me.

The toilet was just off the room through a flimsy door. I was desperate for a wee myself but there was no way I was going to go as I knew the security guards and Dean could hear every single noise and I felt very self-conscious.

Eventually we went back and Elliot and his dad carried on playing while Evie sat on my knee.

'I got your postcard, son, and I put it on my wall,' he told him. 'I liked the red in it.'

'I'm sorry I haven't written back to them,' Dean said to me.

He suddenly looked embarrassed. 'You see, the thing is, I can't write.'

'Are you able to read or is that difficult too?' I asked.

He shook his head.

'I can't do either so I didn't know what the kids' cards said.'

I could see he felt ashamed about that and I felt really sad for him. 'I'm sure there must be somebody who can help you with that,' I told him.

I made a mental note to speak to one of the guards about it on the way out.

As the time passed, Evie was getting more and more restless. She twirled my hair around her fingers and kept cupping my face in her little hands.

'Car now,' she said. 'Car now, please.'

After a while she gave up and jumped off my lap and started running up and down the room. I could tell she wasn't frightened or upset, she was just bored at being in this hall with a man she didn't have the slightest bit of interest in. I noticed the security guard look up at the clock on the wall and I realised it was a discreet way of telling us an hour was up and it was time to go.

'Well, I think it's time for us to go,' I said.

'That's a shame,' sighed Dean. He picked Elliot up and gave him a cuddle.

'I love you, son,' he said.

'Bye, Daddy,' he replied.

'Love you too, Evie,' he told her but thankfully he didn't try and give her a cuddle.

I lifted up Evie and whispered in her ear, 'Now let's be nice and say bye-bye to Daddy.'

'Bye bye, Daddy,' she said obediently.

I could tell Dean really did love Elliot and Evie, and I knew that was a big thing for him. Dean had grown up in the care system and I'm sure affection and love weren't something that he'd experienced much of growing up.

'Well we'll probably see you again soon,' I said.

'Yes, I've asked for an assessment to see if I can look after the kids when I get out of here,' he said. 'So the social workers said they'd be coming to see me.'

'Good for you,' I said, pleased that at least one of their biological parents was showing an interest in caring for them.

As we walked out I had a quiet word with one of the guards.

'Mr Maguire was telling me how he struggles to read and write so he couldn't read the cards the children had sent him or write back to them. Is there anyone who can help him keep in contact with them?'

'You could try the National Association of Prison Visitors,' he said, giving me a number.

As we walked back to the car, the children seemed quite cheerful. As they got into their car seats they talked about going home to see Tess, Pete and Sam.

'That's exactly what we're going to do,' I told them.

We broke up the journey on the way back by stopping off in the same town. We went into a café for a quick cup of tea and cake and we managed to feed the ducks again. I needed that break just to clear my head. After the contact visit all sorts of things were whirring through my mind. *Had it gone OK? Could I have done anything to make it go better? Did I say the right things?* But overall I think I was relieved. I was pleased about the visit and thought it had gone really well. My pleasure had come from seeing Elliot enjoying being with his dad, seeing him smile and give and receive affection. I knew how important it had been for him to see his daddy again.

That night we all sat around the table having dinner and I told my kids about what happened.

'Evie and Elliot saw their daddy today,' I said.

'Daddy liked my wellies and Maggie told him I loved his spaghetti bolognaise,' said Elliot proudly.

I could see how much the visit had meant to him and that made it worth it for me.

'Did you have a nice time with your daddy, Evie?' asked Tess.

'I saw the ducks,' was the only thing she said.

That night I emailed my notes over to Simon. 'Overall it was a positive contact visit for Elliot,' I wrote. 'Unfortunately Evie still doesn't seem to want to interact with her dad but perhaps in time, as she gets to know him, she'll start to form a bond with him like her brother has.'

It was such a relief to me as the contacts with his mum had been so horrendously stressful.

A couple of days later I managed to get hold of the Prison Visitors Association and arranged for someone to go into the prison and help Dean compose letters to the kids or read any mail that he was sent. A few weeks later an envelope arrived addressed to Evie and Elliot. It was obviously from their dad as it had his prison name and number stamped all over it in big letters. I'd never received a letter from prison before and I snobbily worried about what our postman must think!

The kids were delighted to get a special letter addressed to them. They eagerly ripped it open and inside were two pictures of Dumbo that their dad had coloured in for them.

'To Evie and Elliot, love Daddy' it said, in a childish scrawl.

Someone else had obviously addressed the envelope for him as it was completely different writing.

'Show Tess and Pete the pictures that Daddy sent you. Aren't they beautiful?' I said.

The kids soon lost interest in them, but I made sure the pictures were stored safely away in their memory boxes.

I was more than happy to take the kids to regular contact with their dad. Evie hadn't got anything out of it but I knew it was so important for Elliot to foster that bond. Seeing him with his dad had also shown me one important thing – it had proved that Elliot could attach to people, which made me even more confident that the kids *were* adoptable if it did come to that. Sadly I knew from experience that it would be hard for their dad when he was released from prison. He wouldn't have a job or anywhere to live, so I suspected it would be doubtful that he would be given custody of both children. If he wasn't deemed suitable then I believed there was real hope that one day they could find their for ever family.

TWELVE

Seeing the Sea

Turning the pages of the book, I pointed out all of the things in the picture.

'That's the beach,' I said. 'You can see the sand and next to it is the sea.'

I was reading Evie and Elliot *Topsy and Tim Go on Holiday* to try to give them an understanding about holidays and going away from home. I needed to get them used to the idea because in October half-term I'd decided to take us all on a minibreak to Eastbourne. We'd go there a few times a year and always stayed at the same little hotel. It was lucky as my kids' half-term break fell a week earlier than most other schools in the country so I knew it would be nice and quiet.

I must admit it was a bit of a leap of faith. Evie and Elliot were just becoming more settled and there was a chance going away might bring back their old insecurities and fears. But I also knew I had to balance that against Tess, Pete and Sam's needs. We hadn't been away at all during the summer holidays, which is when we'd normally go to Eastbourne, and I wanted to do something nice for them. My three had been incredibly good with Evie and Elliot and I didn't want them to get resentful so I felt that we all could do with a change of scene and a break. Also going on holiday was a normal part of family life and something Evie and Elliot needed to get used to. I'd only booked two nights, as I thought that was a manageable amount of time, just in case it all did go horribly wrong and the children were unsettled.

So I'd dug out the Topsy and Tim book and over the next few nights I read it to Evie and Elliot. I knew that they had no concept whatsoever of holidays. They'd never been on holiday and as far as I knew, they hadn't been out of the town where they lived.

'Have you ever been to the seaside?' I asked them and Elliot shook his head.

'Do you know what the seaside is?'

Another headshake and a puzzled look from Evie.

I used the book to try and get them used to some of the things they might see at the seaside, like sand and sea, and the concept of going away from home and sleeping in different beds, which was completely alien to them. One night as I was reading it to them I said casually, 'We're going to go away and see the sea soon just like Topsy and Tim.'

Both Evie and Elliot looked at me suspiciously.

'Are you coming too?' Elliot asked with a worried look on his face.

'Of course I am,' I said. 'And Tess, Pete and Sam. We're all going to go away together.'

My kids were ecstatic when I told them about our little trip away.

'We're going on holiday! We're going on holiday!' Tess and Pete chanted as they jumped up and down with excitement.

Evie and Elliot still looked unsure.

'Can I take my handbag?' asked Evie.

She was obsessed with a purple velvet handbag that Tess had given her and she carried it with her everywhere she went.

'Yes, you can bring your handbag,' I said, which seemed to reassure her.

I ran the idea past Simon too.

'I'm planning to take the kids away for a couple of days to Eastbourne,' I told him. 'Please could you get permission from the local authority for me?'

I also needed to get permission from Jenny about the sleeping arrangements as I was going to be sharing a room with Evie and Elliot.

'I'm sure Jenny will be fine with it,' he said. 'After all, you deserve a break.'

He was right. It had been a challenging three months since Evie and Elliot had come to live with us and I was looking forward to getting away.

As the holiday drew closer, everyone was incredibly excited and soon we were all packed and ready to go. My kids had shown Evie and Elliot buckets and spades and Evie had insisted on taking a couple of pairs of sunglasses for her and Elliot in her handbag. We left at 10 a.m. on the dot, and to keep them occupied during the long journey I put on a DVD for the children to watch in the car. Everything was going fine until we were stuck in traffic on the M25. Tess was sitting in the last row of our people carrier with Evie and suddenly I heard her shouting from the back.

'Urggh, Evie's being sick!'

I looked round to see what I could only describe as a volcano of vomit coming out of Evie. There was nothing I could do as I was driving, but Tess, bless her cotton socks, was grabbing anything she could from the boot to mop it up – coats, blankets, clothes. I'd never seen anything like it and I couldn't believe how much sick was coming out of such a little girl! Thankfully Evie didn't seem upset by it and I suspected this was probably the longest journey she'd ever been on in her life. Although Evie was OK, the car absolutely stank and there was no hard shoulder on this particular stretch of motorway so I couldn't pull over. It felt like the longest journey ever as we crept round the M25 and as soon as we got near some services I stopped off.

I flung the car doors open and the kids all got out the car. I went into the garage and bought some kitchen roll and we used that and lots of baby wipes to clean the car as best as we could. As soon as we got to Eastbourne the first thing I did was find a garage to get the car valeted and then a launderette. I shoved the car seat covers and everything else that was covered in sick into the wash while we went to a nearby café for a drink.

Well that was an unexpected start to the holiday, I thought to myself as I sipped my mug of tea. But things started to look up as soon as we got to the hotel. It was a small hotel in a three-storey house so it was nice and cosy and not too intimidating for the children. I'd been coming here with my kids for four years and the owners, Rita and Dennis, were lovely. They greeted Tess, Pete, Sam and I with a hug and said hello to Evie and Elliot. They knew I was a foster carer and Dennis worked for the local Social Services. We went straight upstairs to unpack and show Evie and Elliot the rooms. They were sharing my room which had a single bed and a double in it. They were only tiny so they were happy going top to tail in the single bed. I wanted them in with me in case they woke up in the night and didn't know where they were and got frightened. Off our room was an adjoining room with three single beds where Pete, Sam and Tess were going to sleep.

So far, so good, Evie and Elliot seemed fine about being somewhere new.

Again they took their lead from the older children and they followed them around the hotel exploring. There was a little playroom and a sitting room so we just decided to stay there for about an hour or so while I unpacked.

My kids couldn't wait to go to the beach so just before dinner we went for a quick walk. It was getting dark so we just had a little wander down the seafront. Evie and Elliot didn't show any reaction, in fact Elliot was more concerned about when we were going to eat.

'Where's our food, Maggie?' he kept asking. 'When will it be coming?'

'Don't worry, we'll have dinner back at the hotel,' I said.

Being away from home meant that all his old insecurities about regular mealtimes had come back, but I did my best to reassure him.

I think both he and Evie were relieved when we went back to the hotel for dinner at 6 p.m. and they couldn't believe their eyes when they realised they were getting a three-course meal.

'Are we really having three dinners?' Elliot asked, his eyes as wide as saucers.

After tea the older children played in the little play area outside while I took the littlies upstairs to have a bath and put them to bed. Thankfully they were both so tired they settled down immediately and slept soundly all night.

The next morning we all had breakfast together downstairs. The dining room wasn't full but there were staff milling around and a few other guests. To make Evie and Elliot feel more secure, I chose a table by the window and sat them side by side facing inwards, with their backs to the glass. That way they could see everyone approaching them from the front. Then I sat my children either side of them so they were their bodyguards protecting them from the rest of the room. Anyone watching us would have thought what well-behaved children they were, but I knew Evie and Elliot were so quiet because they were anxious about being in a new place. They were very wary and watchful but there were no tears or screaming which was a big relief.

After breakfast we walked to the beach. Tess, Pete and Sam were so excited, they went running down to the sea straight away. Elliot and Evie just looked really puzzled and confused. They couldn't understand why my kids were getting so excited.

'That's the sea,' I told them. 'Just like in the Topsy and Tim book.'

But they just didn't get it. They understood that there was lots of water but they couldn't work out what it was.

'It's like a really, really big bath,' Tess tried to explain to them. 'On a hot day you can put on swimming costumes and go in it and when you come out you have big towels to dry yourself with.'

Tess, Sam and Pete took off their shoes and socks and ran back down to the water's edge.

'Come on,' Tess shouted to Evie and Elliot. 'Come and have a paddle. It's fun.'

But no matter how much they tried to persuade Evie and Elliot, they were having none of it. Evie just clung on to my legs and Elliot shook his head.

'No, no, no,' he said. 'No sea.'

They seemed terrified of the beach and the way their shoes sank down into the pebbles as they walked across it. The most I managed to persuade them to do was collect some pebbles and put them in Evie's handbag and we also had a game of skimming stones. It was too cold to stay on the beach for long and Evie and Elliot looked relieved when we left.

The children spent the rest of the morning clambering on some rocks and afterwards we walked down to the harbour and looked at the boats and yachts.

'I'm going to get on that boat and sail to America,' said Tess.

'Well I'm going to be a pirate and go to the Caribbean,' Pete told her.

Evie looked really concerned and she grabbed Tess's arm.

'Me come too,' she said.

She still had no understanding of make-believe and I had to reassure her and Elliot that nobody was really sailing off anywhere.

It was a cloudy, grey day but every time we looked at the sea, Evie would pull both pairs of sunglasses out of her handbag and solemnly hand one to Elliot. Then they'd put them on, look at the sea and take them off. I couldn't understand why she was doing it until later that day I remembered the Topsy and Tim book we'd been reading. In one of the pictures Topsy and Tim were on the beach looking at the sea with sunglasses on and Evie obviously thought that you had to do that every time. I don't think she had any idea why she was doing it but it was what the book said!

To stop the children getting a complex about water, that afternoon I decided to take them all to the swimming pool. It was indoors and heated so I thought they might enjoy a splash around in there a bit more than the cold beach. They got dressed into their swimming things OK and they liked their orange armbands and pink rubber ring but when we walked out to the pool they were very unsure and nervous. My three jumped in straight away and were splashing around but Evie and Elliot refused to get in the water. I sat on the side with them for ages, reassuring them. Finally they agreed to get into the baby pool but neither of them would let go of me.

'Out now,' Evie kept repeating. 'Don't like people in big bath.'

I could see they weren't enjoying it at all so we left after fifteen minutes.

The next day I took them to Brighton which was much more of a success. We wandered around a shopping area called The Lanes and it was lovely and sunny so we sat outside a café and had lunch. There was a man opposite us who was one of those human statues. He was dressed in a silver suit and even his face and body were painted silver. Tess and Pete had seen one of these before so they took Evie and Elliot over to have a look at him. Tess put a pound coin in his hat and the 'statue' suddenly sprang to life, bent down and shook her hand. I should have seen it coming but pandemonium broke out. Both Evie and Elliot jumped a mile and let out blood-curdling screams before legging it back to me. They threw themselves into my arms, sobbing.

'It's all right,' I soothed. 'It's just a silly man pretending to be a statue.'

But they couldn't understand it. The poor bloke was mortified so he came over to us to apologise but that only made things worse. Evie took one look at him and started screaming again.

'No, no, go away!' she yelled.

'Don't like it,' wailed Elliot.

To cheer them up that afternoon I took them to a wonderful chocolate shop café. The children were fascinated by the amazing window displays and decorations all made out of chocolate. As a treat we had afternoon tea there. The decor was incredible and the children couldn't work out what to look at first. There were brightly painted walls, AstroTurf carpet, artificial flowers and ivy trailing all over, with little bunnies and animals poking out of spaces, and the tea was lovely. As a china cake stand arrived crammed with sandwiches, scones and cakes, Evie and Elliot's eyes grew bigger and bigger and we had a lovely few hours in there filling our bellies.

When we came out, it was almost like Elliot was so relaxed he forgot himself for a minute and he happily skipped up the street with Tess and Pete. It was lovely to see him being so carefree and not the worried, anxious little boy that he'd been when he arrived. It also made me feel like bringing them away had been the right decision. We felt a long way from contact visits, meetings and social workers, and it was like a weight had lifted from him. In fact, it'd been lifted from all of us.

Before we left to go back to Eastbourne, I took them to the pier and we looked out at the sea. Evie and Elliot were still not keen no matter what we said. There was a little train that ran from one end of the sea front to the other so we all piled on it. If there were people in the way the driver sounded a horn that went 'beep beep' and by the end of the trip all the children were shouting 'beep beep', even Evie and Elliot. I was so happy to see them joining in with the others and coping with a loud noise that a few months ago would have terrified them.

When we went back to the hotel I put Evie and Elliot to bed and they were fast asleep within minutes. I stayed up with the older children and watched TV. The kids were playing so it was on in the background but I heard someone on a programme talking about 'little victories'. That night I went to bed with a smile on my face thinking about what Elliot and Evie had achieved. They'd coped so well sleeping in a strange place, in a new town with men pretending to be statues and sitting in a café having afternoon tea. Today had been filled with so many 'little victories' for me.

On the way back home, as the children had adapted so well with being away, I decided to stop at Bicester Village. I was mindful that our last visit to a shopping centre had been hellish, but although they stayed closed to me, Evie and Elliot were fine. I bought them all some new clothes except for Pete, who begged me for new trainers, so I took them into a Clarks shop. I couldn't believe it when Evie and Elliot followed Pete's lead and had their feet measured.

'New shoes,' said Evie excitedly, going along the shelves and picking out a pink pair. Elliot even chose himself some trainers.

I was so proud of them that I ended up going with the moment and buying everyone a pair of new shoes, except me. They'd had their feet measured and picked out their own shoes without any fuss, bother or screaming. I was amazed, overjoyed and also very, very poor by this point! It made me realise that in the three months they'd been with me how far they'd come from those terrified, traumatised little children who had arrived on my doorstep.

'We had a wonderful time,' I told Simon when we got back. 'It was only a few days but the children made so much progress and gave themselves permission to relax.'

I'd also come back feeling refreshed; it had been a lovely break for all of us. Little did I know that it was the calm before the storm.

THIRTEEN

Breaking Point

A few days after we returned from Eastbourne, it was back to reality with a bump when the issue of contact with the children's mum reared its ugly head again.

I received a call from Simon.

'Jenny has been in touch to say that she'd like to try something different.'

'Right,' I said wearily. 'What's she suggesting this time?'

He explained that a taxi was going to come round to my house where Jenny would be waiting and she was going to take Evie and Elliot in the cab to see their mum at a contact centre.

'I'm not being unhelpful but I don't think that's going to work,' I told him. 'The only thing that slightly reassures the children is when I go with them for at least a part of the visit. What does Jenny think that will achieve?'

'She feels that if the kids are away from you then they might be more willing to go in and see their mum.'

Simon explained that Jenny felt the kids were too attached

to me and that was why they refused to go to contact visits. I could feel my hackles rising.

'Of course they're attached to me, Simon,' I said. 'That's my job.'

My firm belief was that children could only grow if they were attached. Evie and Elliot were like babies in their development because that's where they were emotionally. They reacted like an eight-month-old does when its mummy leaves the room. They wanted to be with me all the time and wouldn't let me out of their sight. I felt that trying to take them to contact without me was going to be disastrous, even damaging, for them.

'I think Jenny's just keen to try new things to see if they work,' he said.

I felt that she was being naive by making me out to be the problem and I was angry at being criticised for the children's attachment to me. I'm someone who sticks to my guns and I still felt we should be listening to the children, especially Elliot who was adamant that he didn't want to see his mum. But Jenny didn't seem prepared to hear my concerns.

I was dreading the contact day but I knew it was something that I had to do. As always, I didn't tell Evie and Elliot until right before Jenny was due to arrive to try and minimise their distress. I'd asked Pam our cleaner to come round for a cup of tea and to keep an eye on the older kids in the kitchen so I could focus all my attention on Evie and Elliot. They were watching CBeebies when I mentioned it to them as I thought it would be good for them to have a distraction.

'Guess what?' I said. 'Jenny's coming round in a minute and she's going to take you to see Mummy.'

They were both engrossed in *Balamory*, but Elliot immediately turned round and said, 'I don't want to go.'

'Well we'll have a chat with Jenny when she gets here and you can tell her how you feel,' I said.

A few minutes later the taxi pulled up outside but there was no sign of Jenny.

'I'm afraid the social worker's not here yet but I'm sure she won't be long,' I told the driver.

It was a local firm that Social Services used and all of its vehicles had car seats in them. Jenny finally arrived and after a polite hello she handed me an envelope.

'Oh, Maggie, I must give you this before I forget,' she said.

'What is it?' I asked.

'We've decided to transfer Evie and Elliot to an in-house foster carer so these are her details. We're hoping to move them by the end of next week.'

I was so shocked, I could hardly take in what she was saying but I knew I couldn't react or get my head around this right now. I had more pressing things to tend to – there was a taxi outside waiting for Evie and Elliot and I was expected to help Jenny get them into it. I put the envelope on the side and knew I'd have to deal with that bombshell later.

I went into the living room.

'OK, kids,' I said. 'Jenny is here and the taxi's waiting outside so it's time for you to go and see Mummy.'

'Who do you think's going to be the easiest?' Jenny asked me quietly and I discreetly motioned towards Evie. Although I knew there was no way Evie was going to go willingly, she didn't have the intense, deep-rooted fear of seeing her mum that Elliot had.

However, as soon as Jenny walked towards Evie, she started screaming. She thrashed around but somehow Jenny managed to pick her up and carry her outside to the waiting taxi.

Elliot ran to the window and watched, anxiety etched all over his face.

'That's my sister,' he whimpered as Evie's screams rang out.

Jenny was trying to strap Evie into the car seat but she was hysterical. She kicked and scratched and lashed out at her. I could hardly bear to watch.

'No, no, no!' yelled Evie.

She made her little body rigid and dropped down into the footwell of the car so it was impossible for Jenny to get her into the car seat.

'Do you want me to take you out to the taxi and strap you in?' I asked Elliot, hoping that might reassure him a little and avoid another scene.

'I'm not going,' he shouted. 'I hate Mummy. I don't ever want to see her.'

Evie was still hysterical and even the taxi driver was getting upset.

'This isn't right,' I heard him say to Jenny. 'You can't do this to a child.'

It was horrendous to watch. Eventually Jenny didn't have much choice but to give up and she carried her back into the house. Evie was still distraught, screaming and crying.

'Right, I'll take Elliot then,' said Jenny.

She went over to try and pick him up but there was no way on earth he was going to let Jenny take him anywhere. He punched, kicked and hit out at her so she couldn't even get near him. His fear was so intense you could physically see it. He looked at me pleadingly.

'I don't want to see her,' he whimpered, exhausted after all the lashing out.

I could see that he was terrified that we were making him go back to her.

I felt so helpless as there was nothing I could do.

It was pandemonium. Both kids were hysterical and then Tess came running out to see what was happening. She burst into tears when she saw how upset Evie and Elliot were.

'Go back into the kitchen with Pam, lovey,' I said.

But I couldn't bear seeing the kids so distressed either and I ran upstairs in floods of tears. My hands were shaking as I phoned Simon.

'Just listen to what's happening in my house,' I sobbed. 'It's not right. These poor children are so distressed and frightened.'

'Tell me what's going on,' he said calmly.

I held the phone out of the bedroom door so he could hear the noise for himself.

'This is destroying them, Simon,' I sobbed. 'How can this be deemed to be in their best interests?'

I was so upset as we'd come back from Eastbourne in such a good place. They'd grown so much in the past few weeks and achieved so much on holiday. All I could think about was Elliot happily skipping up The Lanes, smiling and giggling. Evie choosing shoes and going 'beep beep' on the train. All of that progress was being destroyed in one afternoon. I felt every bit of the children's pain and distress. I was like a mother lioness defending her cubs. As much as the kids had attached to me, I had attached to them, and I couldn't bear seeing them go through this.

'This is just cruel,' I told Simon. 'It's putting all their old fears and insecurities back in their heads. They're hysterical because they're worried they're being taken off to live somewhere else. It's horrific to see them so distressed.'

It was very rare for me to be in floods of tears so Simon knew it had really got to me. I also told him about Jenny telling me the children were being moved to an in-house foster carer.

'Have you thought about talking to the children's solicitor and the guardian about trying to stop this?' he said. 'I can email you their details.'

When children are involved in court proceedings, a solicitor and someone called a guardian ad litem are appointed by the courts to act independently in the interests of the children.

'Good idea,' I said. 'But I can't do anything until later. I can't leave these children screaming downstairs like this. I've got to go back down.'

I hung up on Simon and ran back downstairs. Jenny was still struggling with Elliot.

'Jenny, I just don't think this is going to work,' I said. 'You need to stop this now.'

She knew she wasn't going to be able to move either of them on her own and that there was no way on earth I was going to help her manhandle them into the taxi.

'Well I'll have to phone my manager and tell her the children are uncooperative,' she said, obviously flustered.

'You do that,' I said.

I sat on the settee and Evie and Elliot collapsed into my arms. They were inconsolable, their little bodies shaking with sobs.

'No lady, no more lady,' Evie whimpered.

'I hate Mummy,' Elliot sobbed. 'I don't want to see her.'

All I could do was to stroke their hair and hug them and hope that eventually they would calm down. But when Jenny walked back in the room they started howling again.

'Have you decided what you're going to do?' I asked her.

'We'll leave it for now and I'll have to talk to my manager about what happens next,' she told me. 'I'll see myself out.'

I could feel the children's relief that she was going. I watched Jenny walk outside where she told the taxi driver that he wasn't needed. I could see him giving her a piece of his mind.

'That's not right, lady,' he shouted, shaking his head at her. 'You don't do that to little kids.'

Too right, I felt.

I spent the next few hours glued to the settee. Evie and Elliot were distraught and neither of them would let go of me. I was furious. What had been the point of that apart from leaving the children utterly distressed? They clung on to me for dear life and wouldn't leave my side. Evie kept cupping my face and saying, 'No lady, Mummy. No lady.'

'Don't worry, the lady's gone now,' I reassured her, although I'd not sure she believed me.

I couldn't promise them that this wasn't going to happen again because I didn't know, but I hoped to God that it wasn't. All I could do was comfort them.

My own children took a lot of reassuring too. Tess was very upset and even Pam had been in tears in the kitchen.

'Those poor little kids sounded terrified,' she said.

By teatime I'd managed to calm them down enough to give them some food. It was then I noticed the envelope Jenny had given me earlier sitting on the side in the kitchen. After everything that had happened today, it was the final straw. Surely this afternoon was proof enough that moving Evie and Elliot to a different carer was not in their best interests? I knew I'd be devastated if they had to leave in a couple of days. My kids would be gutted too. It was still up in the air about whether Evie and Elliot would be adopted or fostered long term. If fostering was the agreed option then I was happy to step up and say I was open to keeping them for ever. I loved them, my kids loved them and we didn't really want to let go of them.

As a foster carer, I knew I couldn't let my heart rule my head and my personal feelings weren't a good enough reason to keep the children with me. But professionally I knew it would be disastrous to move the kids now, especially after what had happened today. Their worst fears were that they were being taken away for good and I couldn't let that happen. I was sure that this was purely a cost-cutting exercise. If the kids were moved to an in-house foster carer it meant that Social Services didn't have to pay agency fees like they did if the children remained with me. The only way to try and stop it was by doing something drastic.

Simon had emailed me the solicitor's details as he'd promised, but he didn't know who the guardian was yet. In the past I had very rarely contacted a child's solicitor but I felt too strongly about this not to challenge Social Service's decision. I rang Mr Patel and explained who I was and why I was calling.

'Hello, Maggie, I've heard you're doing an excellent job with the children,' he told me.

'Well if that's the case why have I been told today that Evie and Elliot are being moved to another foster carer?'

I explained how disastrous I thought it would be to move the children at this point.

'As a foster carer I'm supposed to be an advocate for these children and I know it wouldn't be fair on them,' I told him. 'I've seen so much progress in them in the last few weeks and all that would be wasted. They'd be back to square one. They'd be back to the traumatised, terrified little ones they were when they first arrived here. It's about saving money and not about the needs of these children.'

Thankfully Mr Patel seemed to be willing to take my concerns on board.

'Thank you for ringing,' he said. 'Leave it with me and I'll speak to the guardian. I've heard what you've said and I completely agree. Maggie, I can assure you those children won't be moving until court proceedings have finished.'

I tried to put it out of my mind while I concentrated on putting the kids to bed. After the traumatic day they'd had, Evie and Elliot thankfully went out like a light. Later that evening Simon came round, it was for a prearranged meeting but it also meant we could talk about what had happened that day. I was a weeping, wailing mess as I went over Jenny's attempt to take them to the contact visit.

'If I'm upset about what happened then what must those poor children be feeling?' I said.

We also talked about the decision to move the children to an in-house carer.

'If they move the children from me then they'll be right back to square one,' I said. 'It's as simple as that.'

'Well hopefully the guardian will agree with the solicitor and that won't happen,' he told me. 'I think you've put forward a very convincing argument.'

Simon also agreed to act as a buffer between Jenny and I, as I couldn't cope with her any more.

'I agree that the issue of contact with Mum needs to be relooked at as it's causing the children such distress,' he said.

He'd already arranged a meeting between his manager at the agency and Jenny's manager at Social Services to talk about future contact sessions.

By the time Simon left, I was exhausted and emotionally drained. It had been a horrendous day. The worst I'd had since I'd got the kids. I had a quick shower and I was just putting on my pyjamas when I saw again the envelope Jenny had given me about the new foster carer on the bed. I opened it up and flicked through her details but I couldn't bring myself to read them. I had nothing against her, I was just so opposed to the idea of moving Evie and Elliot. I got the profile and ripped it up into tiny pieces and threw it into the bin. I felt sick. What if the solicitor and the guardian dismissed my concerns and decided to support Social Services' decision? By the end of the week, Evie and Elliot would be gone. But I knew I was going to fight tooth and nail to stop that from happening. Those children could not be moved and face more disruption. They had to stay with me. Surely they had to support that?

FOURTEEN

Joy to the World

Christmas is often described as the season of joy and for us that was actually the case! After the terrible attempt at getting the children to see their mum in a taxi I thought we were due some good news, and for once it came.

'Firstly I'm calling to tell you that Evie and Elliot are getting a new social worker,' Simon told me one day when he rang.

'Really?' I gasped.

'Yep, Jenny's found a new job and is leaving so someone else has been appointed.'

A change in social worker wouldn't normally be a good thing as it meant the children would have to get to know someone new. But in this case I thought it was the best possible outcome, as Evie and Elliot didn't have any bond at all with Jenny or have any loyalty towards her. Normally social workers come and say goodbye to the children before they leave but I thought it was pointless.

'I think seeing Jenny would only upset them, especially after what happened the other week,' I told Simon. 'She has no relationship whatsoever with those kids.'

'The new social worker is a man called Andrew,' Simon told me. 'I've worked with him on previous cases and I think you're going to get on well. He's a good bloke.'

Getting a new social worker couldn't have happened at a better time and to be honest it was a huge relief. Jenny and I hadn't hit it off from the start and I sometimes felt that she was working against me rather than with me to try and help the children. I was also pleased that the new social worker was a man as I thought it would be good for Elliot to have a positive male influence in his life.

'The other good news is that both the guardian and the solicitor have agreed with you, and they've told Social Services that the children are not to be moved from your care until the court makes a more permanent decision about their future.'

Both these things were a massive weight off my shoulders and I couldn't wait to tell the children about their new social worker.

'Remember that lady Jenny?' I asked them.

Elliot scowled.

'No more lady, Mummy,' Evie said pleadingly.

'Well, she's gone now and she won't be coming round to Maggie's house again. You've got a new social worker.'

It was nice to be able to reassure them, as her efforts to force them into a taxi had left them distraught for days. We'd meet the new social worker in a few weeks and until then it meant we could relax and enjoy the build-up to Christmas.

Christmas was a big thing in our house and it was a time of year that I absolutely loved. I talked about it with Evie and Elliot but whenever I mentioned Christmas or Santa, they just looked at me like I was mad. I could see they just didn't get the idea of Christmas and it was clearly something they weren't familiar with. Like I'd done with the holiday, I bought them some books about it but whenever I tried to explain about Father Christmas and presents, I was met with blank stares.

'How can they not know about Santa?' asked Tess.

'Well some children are not lucky enough to come from a home where they have Father Christmas,' I said.

I was really looking forward to spoiling Elliot and Evie under the guise of Santa. When children come into care you don't want to overwhelm them by buying them gifts and toys, and it wouldn't have been fair on my kids. I'd bought them a few books and clothes but this was my first chance to get them some things that were just for them. I knew they'd never had their own toys before and they hadn't had their birthdays yet, so this was my first opportunity to really treat them.

But being a single parent, it was always tricky to find the time to get to the shops without the children in tow.

'I'll babysit for you one night and you can go late night shopping,' offered Pam when she came round to clean one day.

A few nights later I took her up on that, and slipped out to Toys R Us when the kids were all in bed. I was like a big kid myself as I went up and down the aisles filling my trolley. I bought Elliot a workbench, lots of Duplo, Spiderman toys and a racing car on a track. I even managed to find him his own set of buttons that he could thread on a string and I was going to put them in a tin exactly like mine. Evie had a Baby Annabell doll, a whole heap of *Night Garden* toys and an easel for drawing. Then there were lots of puzzles, games and books for them both to share. My trolley was piled high and it took me ages to load everything in the car. I went into the house first to open the door so I could sneak all the presents upstairs. But much to my horror, Evie and Elliot were both sat up wide awake with Pam.

'Mummy!' whimpered Evie. 'You back.'

'Sorry, Maggie,' sighed Pam with an apologetic look on her face. 'I'm afraid the minute you left they both woke up and they've been asking for you ever since.'

I couldn't believe it. Normally they went to bed and they were flat out until morning but it was sod's law the one night I'd popped out they'd woken up.

'There hasn't been any screaming, thank God, but they're both very anxious,' she told me out of earshot of the children.

Poor Pam. Every few seconds for two hours they'd been asking where I was, but she was determined not to interrupt my shopping. Neither Elliot nor Evie were very happy and they needed lots of reassurance and cuddles.

'I just nipped out to the shop but I'm back now,' I told them.

'Are you going out again?' Elliot kept asking.

'I'm not going anywhere, darling,' I told him but neither of them looked convinced.

In the end, I gave Elliot my car keys to take to bed, just to prove that I wasn't going anywhere. Even though they'd come so far over the past few months, their old insecurities would emerge every once in a while. Over the next few days they were still very clingy and kept checking that I wasn't going anywhere without them. Elliot even insisted on carrying my car keys with him around the house just to make sure that I was telling the truth!

Soon the countdown to Christmas was in full swing. In early December my agency had a big party at a local hotel for all of its staff, foster carers and their children. I bought Evie some sparkly red party shoes to go with her dress and Elliot had a smart shirt and a new knitted tank top. Amazingly they both coped really well with the party. My kids came along too and they could see that they were enjoying themselves on the dance floor so they joined in too. Like all good Christmas parties, Santa put in an appearance.

'That man in the red suit is Father Christmas,' I told them. 'Just like the one we saw in the books.'

Evie and Elliot just stared at him with huge, frightened eyes. Evie wasn't sure, but she agreed to walk towards him firmly clutching my hand. Elliot was a little braver but neither of them seemed that keen.

As part of the build-up to Christmas, I also booked tickets for a pantomime. There was no way on earth I would have taken Evie and Elliot to a packed theatre filled with hundreds of people as it would have been too much for them. But there was a special performance of Aladdin designed for children with autism like my Sam. I knew it would be perfect for Evie and Elliot too as all the noisy, scary bits had been taken out. There was no loud music, flashes or explosions, it was all very gentle and toned down so there was nothing in it that I thought would upset them. It was still a big risk though.

On the day, we arrived early so the theatre was quiet, and my kids came too so we all sat together in one long row. I was in the middle with Evie and Elliot on either side of me. As the place started to fill up, I could see they were very unsure. Both of them were crawling all over my lap and clinging on to me.

'Sit in your own seat like a big boy, Elliot,' I told him but no matter how hard I tried I couldn't get Evie off my knee.

When the lights went down, I could tell they were anxious but there was no screaming. I think they were able to manage as we had created a little bubble around them. My kids and I were like a brick wall keeping them safe and protecting them from the outside world.

Thankfully they loved it and although I don't think they understood the story they were absolutely mesmerised. Halfway through I looked round and sneaked a look at Elliot's face and he was grinning in delight. He saw my kids laughing and shouting out and, to my amazement, he joined in too.

I couldn't help but smile as I heard his little voice shouting out, 'It's behind you!'

To the outside world we looked like an ordinary family enjoying the panto but this was a momentous moment for Evie and Elliot and yet another sign of how far they'd come.

Ten days before Christmas we put the tree up one Friday night. Every year I got a huge real one delivered. As two delivery men dragged it into the front room for me, Evie and Elliot looked intrigued.

'Why are you putting a tree in our house?' Elliot asked, puzzled.

'Because it's Christmas.' Pete laughed, but I could tell despite all the books and the excited chatter, it was still an alien concept to them and they just thought we were being ridiculous. Even though they didn't really understand why we were doing it, Evie and Elliot both loved helping to decorate it.

'Let's get to work, kids,' I said, handing them some baubles each.

They hung various home-made decorations and baubles on the branches and I helped them set off party poppers so the brightly coloured streamers exploded all over the tree. Then later, when everyone was in bed, I started to transform the front room into a magical grotto. I wound strings of brightly coloured musical lights around the tree, I put snowflake transfers all over the front windows and hung huge baubles on strings from the curtain rail. Every surface had some flashing toy or ornament on it that played a tinny Christmas tune. There was everything from a spinning carousel to a dancing penguin and it was all finished off with a little train on a track that chugged around the bottom of the tree. It was so garish and over the top but I knew the kids would absolutely love it.

The next morning after breakfast I took them all into the front room and showed them the transformation.

'Ta-da!' I said. 'What do you think of our Christmas grotto?'

'Wow,' gasped Elliot.

Their eyes lit up and they all spent ages wandering around looking at all the new things.

By Christmas Eve, my kids' excitement was at fever pitch but Evie and Elliot looked worried and anxious all day.

'What is it?' I asked them before they went to bed.

'I don't want Santa to come in the house,' said Elliot.

'No man,' Evie told me. 'Don't like man.'

So to reassure them, we left out a mince pie, a glass of milk and a carrot for Rudolph but we put it in the porch.

'Look, I'm locking the front door just to make sure Santa won't be coming inside,' I said, showing them.

Thankfully that seemed to reassure them. As soon as they were in bed I quietly bought all the presents down to the front room – it was gone 3 a.m. before I'd finished. By the time I crept off to bed there were five towering piles for each child next to their stockings. I made sure I took a picture of Evie and Elliot's to put in their memory book.

I can't wait to see their little faces, I thought.

I just hoped that my children wouldn't question how Santa had got the presents in if we'd locked the front door.

By 5.30 a.m. Pete was tapping me awake.

'Not yet,' I said. 'You know the rules, 6 a.m. is the earliest we can get up.'

At 6 a.m. on the dot they were all ready to go downstairs. I'm one of those annoying parents who insist on breakfast before presents. There were chocolates and sweets in their stockings and I didn't want them filling up on sugar first. I'd never seen them all eat breakfast so quickly.

'OK, it's time,' I said finally. 'Shall we go into the front room and see if Santa's been?'

Tess took Evie's hand as I'd put their presents near each other and Pete led Elliot into the front room while Sam and I followed behind them. As my kids pushed open the door, they gasped. The three of them immediately ran over to their pile of presents and got stuck in. Soon there were piles of wrapping paper everywhere as they frantically ripped the parcels open. Meanwhile Evie and Elliot just stood there, looking completely confused and bewildered.

'Kids, remember to show Evie and Elliot which one is their pile,' I reminded them.

'Come on, Evie, these are yours,' said Tess, taking her hand and leading her over to her huge heap of presents. She thrust one into her hands.

'Go on,' she said. 'You can open it.'

But Evie just looked puzzled as she turned the box around and around in her hands. Suddenly it clicked. Not only had these poor kids never celebrated Christmas, they'd never clearly had a present given to them either. Neither of them had a clue what to do with it.

'Tess, you show her what to do,' I told her while I led Elliot over to his pile.

Tess got the box and ripped a bit of paper off the corner.

'You rip the paper off then you get to see what's inside,' she said.

Evie still looked unsure as she gingerly tore off the tiniest piece of wrapping paper. Tess helped her with the rest of it and when she saw the Baby Annabell doll she grinned.

'That's for you, Evie, from Santa,' I said but I don't think she realised that these were her toys to keep. Neither her nor Elliot had any expectations about Christmas as they'd never experienced anything like it in their lives before.

Now it was Elliot's turn to learn how to open presents as he was equally unsure about what he was supposed to be doing.

'Watch Evie,' I told him. 'Now you have a go. I'll rip a bit for you, now you pull the rest off.'

He was very cautious at first and I had to help him, but three or four presents in, both kids suddenly got the hang of it. It was lovely to see the smiles on their faces as they ripped off the wrapping paper and oohed and aahed at what was inside.

'More! More!' Evie yelled when she'd finished opening her presents and we all laughed.

'Can we do this again tomorrow, Maggie?' Elliot asked, but I shook my head.

'I'm afraid Christmas only comes once a year, lovey,' I said. 'That's what makes it so special. You can help me open my pressies if you want.'

Elliot nodded. The older children had made me some things at school and Elliot helped me unwrap a little clay pot from Pete and an angel candle holder and an elephant calendar from Tess.

'They're lovely.' I smiled. 'Aren't I lucky?'

At lunchtime we all tucked into turkey with all the trim-mings. It was just the six of us and it was exactly the sort of low-key, peaceful day that I'd wanted for the children. After lunch I handed Evie and Elliot another parcel each.

'Daddy sent these for you,' I said.

A few days before Christmas, I'd had a call from someone at the National Association of Prison Visitors saying they had some presents from Dean to drop off for the children.

'The prisoners earn tokens for doing jobs which they can use to buy privileges like cigarettes or chocolate,' the man who brought them round told me.

But instead of spending his tokens on himself, Dean had used them to get the kids some Christmas presents. I thought it was a lovely thing to do. I could tell Elliot was pleased to get something from his daddy but as expected Evie was less keen. Both children had got used to the idea of presents by now and happily ripped them open. Elliot had a little train in a ball that rolled round the floor and Evie had some colouring books and pencils. There was also a card which I read out to them.

To Evie and Elliot, happy Christmas love Daddy.

We'd heard nothing from their mum, who had disappeared again according to Social Services. To be honest that was a relief to me, as if she wasn't around that meant there would be no contact visits which would give us a bit of breathing space for a while.

The children spent the afternoon playing with their new toys.

'Now later on, kids, you have to decide which toys you want to put in your bedroom and which ones you want to keep downstairs,' I said.

There was a rule in our house that if a toy was downstairs everyone shared it and you couldn't moan if someone touched it but special things were kept in your bedroom.

'What do you think, Evie and Elliot?' I said.

'Please can we keep all of them?' asked Elliot.

'Of course you can,' I said. 'They're yours.'

But I still think neither of them realised that these toys were theirs for them to keep for ever. In the end I decided for them and put most things in their bedroom except Elliot's workbench and Evie's easel which were too big to cart upstairs.

The rest of the day was exactly as I'd hoped it would be – quiet and relaxing. We all snuggled up on the settee and watched a DVD. By 6 p.m., I looked across at Evie and realised she was fast asleep.

I think all that excitement has taken its toll. I smiled as I carried her upstairs.

She was so exhausted she didn't even wake up when I changed her into her pyjamas. Elliot stayed up an hour later but he was so exhausted that he let me carry him upstairs to bed. We were all shattered after our 6 a.m. start and I slept like a log.

The next morning I woke up with a start and looked at the clock in a panic – 8 a.m. Why had Evie not been in and woken me up? Every day like clockwork she normally ran into my room just after 7 a.m. I quickly put my dressing gown on and ran out onto the landing. Evie and Elliot's door was open and, much to my relief, I could hear chattering and laughing coming from their bedroom. I peeped in and saw the pair of them sitting on the floor happily playing with their Christmas toys.

To hear the contended chitter-chatter coming from their bedroom was just lovely. It was the first time they'd had any toys to call their own and it was nice to see them having that pride and sense of ownership in their things. It was also wonderful to see them playing independently. There was no one else there showing them what to do or guiding them, they were just playing naturally like children do. It made me realise that all those weeks of patiently showing them how to play had worked. No matter how frustrating it had been sometimes, it was worth it in the end.

They seemed so happy and content I didn't want to interrupt them so I went back to bed with a cup of tea and a big grin on my face. As far as Christmases go, this had been a good one and for the first time in a long while it really felt like the season of peace and goodwill in our house.

FIFTEEN

Sock Wars

There was a knock at the door and I ran to answer it.

'That will be Andrew,' I said to Evie and Elliot.

It was the new year and this was our first meeting with the new social worker who'd been appointed after Jenny had left. Much to my amusement, my first impression of Andrew was that he was another version of Simon.

'Nice to meet you, Maggie,' he said, shaking my hand. 'Now where are Evie and Elliot who I've been hearing so much about?'

He was a good twenty years younger than Simon and dressed in jeans and a jumper rather than the hippy clothes that Simon liked, but they both had a similar solid, calm presence about them.

Andrew was keen to meet the children straight away. I took him through to the kitchen and he immediately got down on the floor and started playing cars with them. He was very natural and I could see they were intrigued.

'I'll put the kettle on,' I said.

Evie was wary of this strange man at first but I could tell that Elliot was terribly impressed as Andrew whizzed the cars around the mat, making revving noises. Soon both children were joining in with him and he spent a good thirty minutes with them before we had a chat and a cup of tea.

'I'm very impressed with how well the children interacted with me,' he said. 'I didn't expect that. They've obviously come a long way since they've been placed with you.'

Thankfully one of the first things he wanted to talk to me about was the contact visits.

'I know one of the issues that you're concerned about is contact with Evie and Elliot's mum.'

'Yes,' I said. 'Just before Christmas things reached breaking point. The children just don't want to see her and it's causing them huge amounts of upset and distress.'

'Well, you're with the children 24/7 so I think it's important that we take your views on board,' he said.

I was so pleased that he wanted to hear my opinion about things.

'I know my manager at Social Services has been talking to Simon's manager at your agency and both of them feel that the issue of contact with the children's mother needs looking at again.

'Despite a number of chances, Mum has proved unreliable at the best of times about even turning up to see the kids, so we're going to recommend to the courts that it's not in Evie and Elliot's best interests to keep pursuing regular contact.'

It was a massive relief to know that they wouldn't have to go through that trauma and distress week in week out.

'Before we do that, though, I'd like to ask the children what they think about seeing their mummy,' he said.

'Of course,' I told him.

Elliot must have overheard what Andrew said because he suddenly piped up, 'What did you say? Do we have to see Mummy?'

Andrew got off his chair and sat down with him on the floor.

'What do you think, Elliot? Do you want to see her?'

'No,' he said firmly.

'Evie, would you like to go and see your mummy again?'

'No, thank you,' she said very politely and then carried on playing.

He'd heard it straight from the horse's mouth and I hoped Andrew could see the children were not being influenced by me in the slightest.

'I'll report all of this back to my manager and we'll let you know the outcome,' he said.

Andrew was a breath of fresh air and I was confident that the children and I were going to have a good relationship with him.

As it happened, there were other developments that led to contact with Mum being stopped much sooner than I had hoped. A few days after Andrew's visit the children's guardian rang me for the first time. Her name was Mary and I'd worked with her before on previous cases. She was a lovely lady in her fifties who was very involved and dynamic and I knew she was a good person to have on side.

'I've heard positive reports about the placement so far, Maggie,' she said. 'How are you finding things?'

'Well, the children are making good progress,' I said. 'They've still got a long way to go but they're completely different kids from the terrified, traumatised pair that arrived on my doorstep in the summer.'

I told her we'd had a great Christmas and that the children's father had sent Evie and Elliot some presents.

'I thought if you were speaking to him as part of his assessment then you might be able to pass on the message that we got them and the children were very pleased.'

'Ah, well, there have been a few recent developments that I need to tell you about,' she said. 'I'm afraid Dad's assessment has been cancelled.'

'What happened?' I asked.

Mary explained that Dean had recently been given early release from the open prison but a few days later he'd been involved in a violent incident at the hostel where he was living.

'It breached the terms of his parole so he's been sent back to prison to serve the remainder of his sentence.

'Also the psychological reports on both parents have come back and it's clear that neither of them can meet the needs of the children,' she continued.

A psychologist had assessed both Sheena and Dean. She'd recommended that Sheena had counselling but she'd refused to do that. Her conclusions about Dean were that he didn't have any concept of the impact the domestic violence and his drinking had had on the children.

'Apparently he blames everything on his ex-partner and her suicide attempt, and sees it as her failure to look after the children properly,' continued Mary.

'The psychologist strongly felt that neither parent would be able to maintain good enough care for Evie and Elliot because they're not willing to address their own problems. We feel that adoption is the best possible outcome for the children, so that's what we're focusing on now.'

Listening to all that, I felt sad that neither of their parents were willing to take responsibility for their actions and see the harm they'd caused. But I was pleased about the adoption.

'That's great news,' I said. 'Especially as the previous social worker was very against it.'

'Well, we've moved on now, haven't we?' she said.

As much as I was attached to Evie and Elliot, I knew adoption was the best possible option for them. They deserved to grow up in a for ever home rather than a foster home. I'd always known adopting them wasn't a possibility for me because my job was being a foster carer. The sad fact was I couldn't afford to adopt them as then I'd have to give up fostering or limit my numbers and it would be a struggle to pay my mortgage.

'I think adoption is the right thing,' I agreed.

Three weeks later the courts granted a full care order and a freeing order, which meant that Social Services were now the legal guardians of Evie and Elliot and they were free to be put up for adoption. Neither of their birth parents was in agreement with that and each of them had refused to meet with Social Services to discuss their feelings and wishes for the children.

Although the children had come on in leaps and bounds I knew that Elliot in particular had lasting trauma and we still had a lot of work to do. His anxiety was always there, bubbling away under the surface, and sometimes it came out in different ways. There was one strange way in particular – around this time he developed a bizarre obsession with socks. It started one morning when I asked him to go and put some socks on.

'Your feet will get cold on the tiled floor,' I said. Also if we decided to go out later it was much quicker if his socks were already on rather than having to go back upstairs and find them. But Elliot wasn't happy about it. He went thumping up the stairs, stamping his feet on every step.

'What's wrong with him?' asked Tess, but I had no idea.

I followed him upstairs as I had a pile of clean towels to take up to the bathroom. As I was putting them away, I heard Elliot opening and closing all his drawers.

'What's wrong?' I shouted.

'I haven't got any socks,' he yelled.

I always got the children to take bits of clothing upstairs to put away when it was washed and dried as this gave them a sense of ownership and control.

I bet he's put his socks in the wrong drawer, I thought.

'Do you want some help?' I called out.

There was no answer so I went into his bedroom and pushed open his door. Elliot was sitting in the middle of the floor cross-legged and very cross. I opened the drawer that had his socks in.

'Look, they're all here,' I said. 'Do you want me to choose you a pair?'

I thought perhaps he couldn't work out which ones to wear.

'No!' he shouted.

'Do *you* want to choose a pair then?'

'No, no, no!' he yelled.

I didn't understand what the problem was so I left him to it. Five minutes later he came downstairs and played with some Duplo while I folded up more washing. I hoped his strop was over so I picked up a clean pair of socks and thankfully he allowed me to put them on his feet. But then the complaining started.

'They're too tight, Maggie. They're hurting my feet,' he moaned.

'They're absolutely fine,' I replied.

'They're not, they're really ouchy and scratchy.'

'Elliot, they're fine,' I told him.

But in a fit of rage, he ripped them off and threw them on the floor. I'd never seen him so cross.

'Do you want to go upstairs and choose a different pair?' I asked him, but he didn't respond.

I wasn't going to get involved and when we went out later Elliot put on his wellies with no socks.

'Are you sure you're fine in those and no socks?' I asked and he just grunted.

Sometimes you have to pick your battles, and if Elliot wanted to go out sockless then I wasn't going to stop him. However, from then on the silly issue of socks triggered some amazing temper tantrums from Elliot. This was different to his usual upset. It wasn't hysterical screaming or tears, it was pure and utter anger and rage. Socks became a big problem for him whenever he was faced with a new situation or felt anxious.

As always, I talked it through with Simon.

'I think it's all about control,' I said. 'Perhaps it's because he feels he has no choice or control over anything else in his life.'

It was also about what they represented. You put your socks on if you were going out so I think Elliot thought if he didn't have socks on then maybe we would stay in the safe place that was home. Choosing a pair could literally take hours, so I'd bring a huge washing basket full of different pairs in every single size and colour and let him decide while I was driving. He used not putting his socks on to try and avoid doing something he didn't want to do. One weekend I decided to take everyone to the local soft play centre that they loved. But in the car Elliot kicked off and refused to choose a pair of socks from his basket. I'd worked out by then it was because he was anxious about going somewhere or doing something, but I was determined he wasn't going to control me. As I pulled up into the car park I said, 'Elliot, you need your socks on to go into the soft play.'

'No!' he said defiantly.

'OK then, I'll count to five and you'll get your socks on otherwise you'll miss out on what the others are doing. They can go and run round the soft play but I'll stay with you at the side and watch. Is that what you want to happen?'

Elliot shook his head and begrudgingly started to pull on a pair of socks. Sometimes he had to see where he was going and be reassured in order to move forward.

It was times like that that reminded me that Elliot was still a deeply anxious little boy. I knew he was going to be tested even more over the coming months as my main aim for the new year was to get both him and Evie settled into preschool. I was very aware that Elliot was turning four soon, and in September he was due to start primary school. I knew it was important that he felt secure enough to be apart from me for a couple of hours at least otherwise there wasn't a hope in hell that he was going to start school without a battle. But so far Elliot had never been apart from me and I was worried about how he was going to react. Would he be able to cope with going to nursery? Or would the frightened, terrified, hysterical little boy who arrived on my doorstep be back?

SIXTEEN

Separation

At the end of January I took the children for a look around the local preschool. I didn't give them a choice about it, I just presented it as a normal thing that children their age did and so they were going to do it.

I thought it was important for both of them to mix with their peers and to get used to being away from me, especially Elliot. I knew it would be helpful for him to try and have a little group of friends or at least other children he would recognise when he went to big school in September.

'Do you think the kids are ready for it?' asked Andrew when he came round for a meeting.

'I think so,' I said. 'At least I think we need to try it.'

Evie and Elliot were at a point where they were having more and more contact with the outside world. They'd had months of just being at home with me and settling in, which they'd desperately needed. Now, although they were still fearful and anxious at times, I was able to manage it more and I could catch it before it escalated into a full-scale episode. Normally

I found the easiest tactic was to distract them by saying something completely random and ridiculous, like, 'Ooh I wonder if I've put all my toes on today!' Then I'd start counting them. Evie and Elliot would either laugh or look at me like I was completely mad but it would normally do the trick and diffuse a traumatic situation.

One morning I decided to take the bull by the horns.

'We're going to go to the preschool in the village today and have a look around,' I said.

'Why?' asked Elliot.

'Because you and Evie need to go to preschool because that's what children your age do. Pete, Tess and Sam all go to school and now it's your turn.'

I knew neither of them had a clue what a preschool or a nursery actually was but they understood the concept of the older children going out to school so they seemed happy to go along with it.

Our nearest one was based in a church hall a few minutes' drive away. As I pushed open the huge doors, the noise was deafening and I could feel Elliot recoil. It was set in two huge rooms and there were thirty children tearing about, playing and laughing. There were lots of toys and games set out and different activities going on in different corners so the children could choose what they wanted to play with. It was busy, noisy and messy and I could tell by the massive smile on Evie's face that she absolutely loved it.

'This is brilliant, isn't it?' I said to her and she grinned back at me.

As soon as she clapped eyes on the huge fancy dress corner with rails of princess dresses, bags of wings and piles of tiaras and crowns, she ran off to explore. Elliot meanwhile clung on to my hand for dear life, his body language screaming, *Please don't leave me here.*

It was like he and Evie had reversed roles. She was normally the hip hugger, as I called her, but she was happily off playing while Elliot clung onto me like a limpet. I could tell that he didn't like it and he didn't feel safe here. I knew instantly this wasn't the right place for him and he would never settle.

'Shall we find you somewhere less noisy?' I said and he nodded.

Whereas Evie was in her element, tearing around, Elliot needed somewhere much smaller, calmer and more nurturing. But what that meant was splitting the children up and I wasn't sure if that was a good thing. Throughout everything they'd been through so far they'd always had each other to cling on to. They were the one constant in each other's lives.

I rang Simon that afternoon and talked it through.

'I'm worried that I'll traumatise them by sending them to different nurseries and it might mean they'll never settle.'

'But remember when Elliot starts primary school Evie won't be with him, so it's important that they both get used to that,' Simon pointed out.

I knew he was right but would they be able to cope with being apart?

'You never know, perhaps it will do them good not to be so dependent on each other,' he said.

I hoped he was right. I knew that Elliot needed to feel confident and safe and the local preschool wasn't going to work for him although it was ideal for Evie's needs.

Luckily they had space, so Evie was able to start there straight away. It was a morning session for two and a half hours every day. On her first day, Elliot and I stayed with her but she was off playing happily on her own. After an hour, her key worker Sian suggested that we leave her to it.

Although I could tell she liked it there, I knew Evie was going to blow a gasket when it came to me actually leaving her and I wasn't wrong.

'Elliot and I are going to go now but we'll come and pick you up in a little while when you've finished playing,' I told her.

She burst into tears and clung on to me.

'Don't go, Mummy,' she sobbed.

I didn't like to see her like that but I'd expected it and I knew it wasn't real distress or anxiety. It was just a cry of protest that I was leaving her rather than something that was going to be a lasting trauma for her.

'Don't you worry, I'll be back soon when all the other mummies come,' I soothed.

I knew a quick goodbye was the best way, so I literally transferred her from my hip to Sian. Elliot watched intently as I handed Evie over. He grabbed my hand and squeezed it tightly, just in case I was entertaining any ideas about leaving him there too.

'She'll be absolutely fine,' Sian reassured me. 'Mark my words she'll be playing happily in ten minutes.'

Earlier she'd discreetly shown me a way of going round the back of the hall and into the toy cupboard. There, between the boxes of toys, you could see into the hall. So when we'd left Evie, Elliot and I sneaked round there just to check that she was OK. As I peered through the gaps in the shelves I could see Evie happily helping herself to some crackers and cucumber from the snack table. I smiled to myself as I knew she'd love being able to help herself to food. The crying had stopped and she seemed absolutely fine so Elliot and I walked into the village and had a drink in a café before we went back to pick her up.

Evie settled in so well that by the third day she was doing a full session. That morning, after I'd dropped her off, I took Elliot to look around a playgroup that I'd heard about in a nearby village. As we pulled up outside, I had a good feeling about it. It was set in a beautiful Victorian house and it seemed very peaceful as there were only twelve children in each session.

'Isn't it nice and calm?' I said to Elliot as we walked in. 'I think you're going to like this one.'

Still I could feel his little hand clinging on to me anxiously.

As we looked around, I could see this place would suit Elliot down to the ground. It was more routine based than Evie's, which was more of a free-for-all. The children could still choose what they wanted to do but it was structured around activities on tables and chairs. Evie had got the hang of imaginative play: she pretended to be a princess and invented stories and acted out role plays with dolls. Elliot didn't have that spontaneity and he still needed to be directed and encouraged in his play.

'Look there's a garden outside,' I said, sounding as enthusiastic as possible. 'And some chickens and rabbits. Ooh look, Elliot, aren't they lovely?'

The children could help grow vegetables and look after the animals and there was sand and water play. After we'd been there a little while, Elliot got the confidence up to join in and he did a bit of digging in the soil.

Although I knew he was still feeling anxious, I could tell his anxiety level wasn't as high as it had been at Evie's nursery, and his body language told me he was a lot more accepting of this place.

'I think it's perfect for you here,' I told him. 'This is the one you're going to come to.'

As part of my plan, I deliberately made the next few mornings with me really dull. After we'd dropped Evie off, I made sure we went home to an empty house and did boring jobs in the hope that it would encourage Elliot to go to preschool and know he wasn't missing out on anything at home.

I knew that he was going to take a lot longer to settle in than Evie, and the staff suggested doing it gradually over a couple of weeks. I stayed with him for the whole of the first session but I just sat in the corner and didn't join in.

'I'm going to sit here and read my book so you go off and play,' I told him.

If I'd gone round with him and started playing then it would have confused Elliot and he'd think that was how it was going to be and then be even more upset when I eventually left him. So I just sat in the corner pretending to read my book, but actually I was constantly watching and checking that he was OK. A few times I felt him brush past me and he kept calling out to me.

'Maggie, come and see this,' he yelled.

I looked up and gave him a smile but then shrugged and pointed to my book. It was so hard pretending to be disinterested but I knew it was important for him to understand that preschool was a place that he went to without me and I had to encourage his independence. Seeing me leave Evie at her nursery had helped make him realise what was going to happen but I was still dreading the second day when I was due to leave him for an hour. I just didn't know how he was going to react.

'Today I'm going to leave you for little while,' I told him gently. 'But I'll be back in an hour.'

'Where are you going?' he asked me.

'Don't you worry, I'm only going to be outside in the car park,' I said. 'I'll sit in my car and read my book so I'll be here if you need me.

'Here, you take my car keys,' I told him.

They were the special ones that I'd had made that were identical to mine to give him extra reassurance that I wasn't going anywhere.

As I gave Elliot a kiss and a cuddle goodbye, I could feel his little body shuddering with fear. The poor little mite was scared stiff but bless him he was being so brave and he managed not to cry.

As much as I was confident that Elliot had moved on, I couldn't help but worry whether he'd moved on as much as I thought. My worst nightmare was that sending him to preschool would send him right back to square one.

His key worker Debbie took him to the door with me so he could say goodbye. There was a panel of glass in it and I could see his little face peeping through it watching me like a hawk as I walked to my car.

I did exactly as I'd promised him. I sat in my car in the car park but I was too nervous to concentrate on reading. I didn't want him to get back to that heightened fear level and start screaming. I knew when he was like that he was inconsolable and if that happened the nursery would then become a trigger for such behaviour and we would have that screaming every single day. If I drove home it would take me a good fifteen minutes to get back and, even if the nursery phoned me, I knew he would be hysterical by the time I got there. I knew it wasn't fair on Elliot either. We'd built up our relationship and he trusted me, believed in me and relied on me. I couldn't let him down.

Over the last six months I'd exposed him to new situations and new people and eventually he'd coped. But was this too much? Also, with all those new things, the key was I'd always been there by his side to help him. Could he really cope with doing this on his own or would he feel rejected and abandoned all over again?

All these worries whirred round my head as I sat in my car. As I stared at the nursery door, I couldn't stop myself reaching for my mobile phone.

I had to check that he was OK.

'He's fine,' Debbie told me. 'We had a few tears at first but he's OK now.'

The call reassured me too because I knew that, if Elliot was really hysterical, his screaming was so loud I'd be able to hear him down the phone.

But I couldn't stop myself from calling a second time fifteen minutes later.

'He's still fine,' laughed Debbie. 'Are *you* OK?'

'To be honest I'm a bit wobbly,' I said.

By the third time I knew I was being completely ridiculous but I just couldn't help it.

'Honestly, Maggie, he's OK,' she said. 'He's very quiet but he's fine.'

It was such a relief.

The staff probably thought I was barmy and that I was being a completely overprotective parent but they didn't know what Elliot had been through. They knew I was his foster carer but for confidentiality reasons I couldn't tell them anything about his past history or how he'd been. I'd have done anything to make sure that he didn't go back there.

I made sure that I was the first mum there at pick-up time as I knew all the children ran to the door and peeped through the glass and I wanted Elliot to see me there first. He was sitting on the floor with the others having story time when I first walked in and I waved at him through the glass. His little face lit up and he wiggled his fingers back at me. It was a tremendous relief.

Over the next few days Elliot slowly settled into his new preschool. He was still very stiff and reserved when I left him but his fear and anxiety had lessened. He'd developed a good relationship with Debbie which I was pleased about and he stuck to her side like glue.

Every day I left him for a little bit longer and eventually he realised that he was safe and that I would always come back for him. The first week I sat in the car park every day after I'd dropped him off, just in case, and much to the staff's amusement I kept calling to check on him. But by the end of the first week I knew I had to be the brave one. I had to summon up the courage to leave him properly and go back home.

Whenever I left I always gave Elliot his special set of keys and they were like his security blanket. But I was also keen not to deceive him.

When I said goodbye he'd ask, 'Where are you going?'

I didn't want to lie to him and pretend I was always going to be sitting in the car park.

'Today I'm going to go home because I've got a bit of sorting to do,' I said. 'But don't worry, Debbie can always phone me and I can come straight back.'

Elliot nodded sadly as if he was resigned to the idea. Funnily enough he never questioned how I could leave without my car keys. But I think even if he'd worked out they weren't my real keys, he didn't care. They'd become a way for him to manage his anxiety.

Over the next few weeks the children settled in well. Although she kicked up a fuss every morning when I dropped her off, I could tell Evie loved her nursery. When I went to pick her up it was like she ruled the roost. 'I'm going now,' she'd announce to everyone in a loud voice.

She was very proud of the fact that she had some little pals and she'd talk about her friends whenever she could. 'Oh my friend's got that toy,' she'd casually drop in a conversation, or, 'My friend likes cheese too.'

Elliot, as always, was a lot more reserved. I tried to talk about preschool at home as much as I could so it became familiar to him. I'd use the names of the other kids and the staff and talk about the activities they did there.

A major turning point was the half-term holiday, at the end of which Evie got chicken pox, closely followed by Elliot. It meant both of them were off nursery for weeks and I was dreading settling them back in. However, much to my amazement, they both started asking about when they were going back.

'School today please, Mummy,' said Evie one morning.

'Are we going back to school soon?' Elliot asked.

It was lovely to hear them asking to go as it meant they liked it there. Being at home for a few weeks with me had made them realise how boring it was and how much more fun going to preschool was.

I needn't have worried about them settling back in. They both walked straight in without any fuss and from that moment on, there were never any tears or worries at drop-off.

Another big turning point for Elliot was when he told me that he'd made a friend. 'He's called Ethan,' he said proudly.

'Well, would you like to invite your new friend Ethan round for lunch one day?' I suggested.

Elliot was delighted when he and his mum came back to our house after nursery one day. Elliot didn't really play with Ethan but he played alongside him. Ethan had only just turned three and he seemed to have more in common with Evie and the pair of them played beautifully together. In a way I think Ethan was a substitute Evie for Elliot at nursery but that didn't matter. What mattered was that Elliot 'got' the idea of having a friend and was happy for someone new to come and visit us at home.

So, with the children settled into their preschools, it meant that I had a couple of hours to myself on a morning. I can't deny that was lovely. At first having Elliot and Evie had been like having newborn babies and I was pretty much tied to the house 24/7. I didn't begrudge that at all as I knew how much they'd needed it, but having some time to myself again felt very freeing. I could go for a coffee and have an adult conversation with other foster carers, and go on some training courses that my agency had suggested. Overall I felt happy and that I'd made the right decision. Sending them to preschool had been the right thing to do. It was more important than ever that they were able to cope with change as they were about to embark on one of the biggest changes in their little lives so far – the long road to adoption and to finding them a new mummy and daddy.

SEVENTEEN

Dropping a Bombshell

As a foster carer, one of the hardest things that I ever have to do is break the news to a child that they're never going to see their biological parents again. It's a massive thing for any youngster and you never know how they're going to react. Even kids who have been neglected or abused are sometimes distraught at the thought they will never see their mummy and daddy again. My challenge is always to try and do it as positively as possible. It was always hard as it wasn't as if the children had any control over this. Other adults had made the decision for them and even though it'd been made in their best interests, it still can cause a lot of upset.

I genuinely didn't know how Evie and Elliot were going to take the news about saying goodbye to their parents for good. I hoped that it would be a huge relief for Elliot not having to see his mum again, and although Evie was a bit more willing Mum was still a virtual stranger to her. Elliot's sticking point would be his dad. He liked this man and had a connection to him but it had been so long since he'd been in the same house as him and I was hoping that he didn't harbour any thoughts about going back to live with him. They were settled with me now and I'd shown them a different life. A life where they had clean sheets and clothes and meals on the table three times a day, and people who cared for them and wanted them. But even still, I could never second-guess children and I didn't know how they were going to react to this momentous news.

My heart was in my mouth when Andrew came round that morning after breakfast. It was the best time of day as the children were less tired and would be more likely to take in what we were telling them.

'I think it's best if you tell them and I'll back up what you're saying,' I said. 'They're more likely to believe it coming from a social worker as they know you and Jenny were the ones who sorted out of the contact visits.'

'I agree,' he said.

Somehow it made it more real and official if the news came from him. I knew if we sat the children down at the table they would be all fidgety and not really take in what we were saying. So we sat on the floor and did a puzzle together as that way I knew they'd be more relaxed. Evie, as always, plonked herself on my lap.

'Elliot and Evie, listen carefully to Andrew as there's something very important that he needs to tell you,' I said.

'We all had a meeting,' he said. 'Maggie was there and Simon and I. We all know that when you go and see your mummy it makes you really upset. So we've decided that you won't be living with Mummy and Daddy any more.

'We're going to organise for you to see them one last time to say goodbye, but after that you don't ever have to see your mummy and daddy or live with them again.'

Elliot obviously heard the words 'see Mummy' and panicked.

'No, I don't want to see Mummy!' he shouted.

I reached out for his hand.

'Elliot nobody's saying that you have to see Mummy again,' I said gently. 'Listen to what Andrew is telling you.'

I knew he always responded well to humour so I tried to make a joke out of it.

'I tell you what,' I said. 'Do you want to borrow my listening ears? I'll get them out of my pocket and lend them to you so you can hear Andrew properly. I think you forgot to put yours on this morning.'

Elliot giggled as I pretended to rummage around in my cardigan pocket. My silly joke gave him a little bit of time and space to concentrate on what Andrew was saying. It was my way of subtly telling him: 'You really need to hear this.'

'So as we were saying, you're going to do one last visit to see your mummy and daddy and then you won't see them ever again,' he continued.

'They love you lots and lots,' I told them. 'But they're not able to look after you and give you clean clothes in your drawers and nice sheets on your bed and warm dinners and take you to nice places.'

I wanted to point out all the things that were new to them when they came to my house. Andrew and I looked at the children and waited for their reaction.

Elliot looked very serious for a moment.

'I don't have to see Mummy ever again?' he asked.

I shook my head.

'I don't have to see Mummy!' he said triumphantly, his face breaking into a huge smile of joy. 'I don't have to see Mummy!'

He was literally jumping with happiness and relief but I wanted to make sure that he'd heard it all.

'Or Daddy, Elliot,' I said. 'After we've said goodbye to him you won't see Daddy ever again.'

'That's OK,' he said.

I turned to Evie. She hadn't shown any reaction to the news and she just looked confused. She glanced up at me and gently stroked my cheek.

'But you're my mummy,' she said.

I suddenly realised that she thought we were saying she couldn't see me again. As far as Evie was concerned, I was her mummy and she'd already transferred her attachment. Poor little thing looked scared out of her wits.

'Not me, Maggie mummy,' I said. 'We mean your tummy mummy. *That* mummy. We'll go and see her and say goodbye then you won't see her again.'

I could see the relief on Evie's face when she realised that it wasn't me she was saying goodbye to. She had no relationship or connection with her dad so I knew that part of it wouldn't bother her.

'What we have to do next is go and see Mummy and Daddy one last time to say goodbye to them, and then after that you'll never have to see them again. Is that OK?'

Elliot nodded and Evie gave me a little smile.

'Can we go out in the garden and play now?' Elliot asked.

'OK,' I said. 'Get your shoes on and off you go.'

I could see the news had been a massive relief to him and it was like a weight was off his mind.

'Well how do you think that went?' asked Andrew, when the children had gone outside.

'I'm pleased,' I said. 'I think it went as well as it could have done. I think they've both taken the news in and it will take them a few days for it to sink in. But overall, I think it's a relief for them. You could see how happy Elliot was.'

Both Andrew and I agreed that the goodbyes with their biological parents needed to be done as soon as possible while the news was still fresh in the children's minds.

'I'd like to take them to say goodbye to Dad first if we can,' I told him. 'I think it's important for Elliot to have the more positive experience first. It will make him more likely to go to the goodbye with Mum. Without that I think we're going to struggle to get him there.'

Andrew explained that Dean had been sent to a high-security prison to finish the remainder of his sentence.

'I know my manager's concerned that it will be too traumatic to take the children in there to see him. What do you think?'

'Even if he's not in the open prison any more I think it's hugely important,' I said. 'Prison or not, Evie and Elliot need that closure.'

Saying goodbye was massively significant for kids and was a way of killing off any of their fantasies or worries. If they didn't say goodbye, some children believed that their parents would come back for them one day, and in Elliot and Evie's case that wasn't hope it was fear. To enable them to move on properly they needed to say goodbye and close the door on that part of their life.

'Saying goodbye will be reassurance for them that they'll never return to their parents,' I told Andrew. 'Only then will they be able to move on properly with a new adopted family.'

Andrew could see how strongly I felt and he was willing to back me up that this goodbye needed to happen.

'As far as I know the visiting orders are already in place,' he told me.

'OK,' I said. 'Well in that case I think I should take the children as soon as possible.'

Evie's smile was as wide as her face as she skipped up and down the shop proudly modelling her new shoes. They were blue leather with a little dolly hidden in the sole, which she loved. Elliot ran alongside her in the trainers he'd chosen which had lights on the side that flashed when he stomped his feet.

'Lovely,' I told them as I went to the till to pay. 'Now let's put them back in the box then tomorrow you can wear them when we go and say goodbye to Daddy. I bet he'd like to see your nice new shoes.'

Evie's face fell.

'No,' she said, shaking her head. 'Don't want to see Daddy.'

'Sweetheart, we need to go and say goodbye to Daddy,' I told her. 'Remember it's just one last time, then after that you'll never have to see him again.'

But I knew Evie was going to take a bit of convincing.

Tomorrow was going to be an important day for them. I'd really had to fight hard for this goodbye with their dad in high security. Social Services were still concerned that it was going to be traumatic for the children to go into the prison but I knew how important it was, especially for Elliot. His mum had constantly rejected him but he idolised his daddy. He was the only person who had ever shown him any affection in the first three years of his life so I knew that saying goodbye was really important for him.

Thankfully, Andrew's superiors had finally seen sense and he'd dropped off the visiting orders that morning. I might have got my way but as I laid out the children's clothes that night, I knew it wasn't going to be an easy day ahead of us tomorrow.

I wanted them to look smart, as it would be the last time their daddy would see them, but be comfortable too, so I'd chosen their favourite 'best' outfits. Evie had a pretty blue smock dress that matched her new shoes and Elliot had a blue cord shirt and a Fair Isle tank top with some navy trousers. I'd deliberately timed the trip to the shoe shop so it would give us a bit of a reason for the visit and something to talk about – we were going to say goodbye to Daddy and show him their new shoes.

The next morning was a bustle of activity as the children got dressed and had their breakfast. I'd tried to present it as a nice day out for them.

'We're going to go to McDonald's for lunch first, then we'll go and say goodbye to Daddy, and afterwards we'll go and find a park so you can have a play on the swings and slides. Does that sound good?'

They both nodded but they were subdued as they tucked into their Weetabix.

I tried to prepare them as much as possible for the prison visit. I'd never actually used the word 'prison' with them because I knew they were too young to grasp the concept.

'Now remember Daddy's in a big building with lots and lots of bricks,' I explained, as I helped get them ready. 'It's a different building to the one we went to see him in a long time ago.'

Even though he'd been close to his dad, Elliot still needed lots of reassurance about the visit.

'Are you coming too?' he asked me.

'Yes,' I said. 'I'm going to come into the building with you and I'll be there all the time.'

'Could Daddy keep me there in the building?' he asked, his blue eyes full of worry.

'No, Daddy won't keep you there,' I told him. 'You'll go in with Evie and me and there'll be other people around. Then we'll say goodbye to him and after that you won't see Daddy ever again.'

Elliot, bless him, wanted to know if he could take him a present.

'I'm afraid we're not allowed to take anything into the building for Daddy but I've got some boxes of juice and a snack for you and Evie.'

The new prison where Dean had been moved was right in the middle of a city centre. It was a long drive there and it took me ages to find somewhere to park. As we pulled up into a side street of terrace houses, I could see its high walls looming in front of us.

'Daddy lives in a castle!' said Elliot.

I could see what he meant. It was a huge Victorian building with almost medieval-style turrets and it was much more forbidding than the single-storey open prison in the middle of the countryside where we'd gone to visit him last time. Once we'd parked we walked around the walls for ages trying to find a way in. Finally we found the entrance and were directed to a waiting room. Evie and Elliot hardly said a word as we sat there, I think the poor things were already exhausted from walking round virtually the whole of the outside of the prison walls. Finally a female prison officer came in carrying a clipboard.

'This way,' she said, ushering us into a curtained area off to one side. 'Before you go in I need to do a body search.'

I was horrified. It was the first time in all my twenty years of being a foster carer that I'd been frisked on a prison visit. Normally, like social workers and solicitors, it was deemed a professional visit and I was able to go straight through without being searched. But I didn't want to kick up a fuss as I knew it would upset the children who were already on edge.

I felt really uncomfortable as the officer got me to stand astride and hold out my arms while she patted me down from top to bottom. Every part of me was poked and prodded, she even had a rummage round under my underwired bra.

'That will set the metal detectors off when you walk through security,' she warned me.

She took my bag from me and confiscated the drinks and snacks I'd brought in for the kids.

'You're not allowed to bring anything in here,' she said. 'You'll get 'em back on the way out.'

But there was worse to come.

'I'm going to have to search the kiddies now,' the officer told me.

I knew the only way to stop them from getting distressed or having a meltdown was to try and make a joke out of it.

'Can you feel his Weetabix in there?' I teased as she patted down Elliot's tummy. 'Or is it just that McDonald's he had for lunch?'

'Ooh, you don't want to go near those smelly feet,' I said as she frisked him up and down his legs.

Amazingly, although he hated physical contact, Elliot seemed fine. Evie was a different matter. As this strange woman came towards her, she leapt into my arms and refused to let me put her down. 'No lady Mummy, no lady,' she whimpered, clinging on to me like a limpet.

'Please can you do it while I'm holding her?' I begged, and thankfully the prison officer agreed.

Evie grabbed fistfuls of my hair and buried her head in my neck as she was patted down.

'You'll have to change her nappy now so we can check that you're not trying to smuggle anything in,' she said.

I'd put Evie in a pull-up as she was only just toilet trained and I didn't know how easy it would be to find a suitable toilet inside the prison. I was thankful the guards were going to let me do it, but two of them watched while I changed her. They took away the old pull-up and then searched the new one to check I wasn't smuggling anything in it before I put it on. Next we each had to walk through a metal detector that kept going off when I went through it. I could see the children flinching every time the loud alarm sounded.

Please don't let them get hysterical and have a meltdown, I thought to myself, as I could see they were getting more and more on edge.

Eventually they worked out it was being set off by a tiny metal bar on my shoes and we were finally allowed to go through into the main prison. I was terrified and bewildered after that experience, never mind the poor kids.

A prison officer led us through into a corridor.

'Because it's special circumstances we've found you a nice quiet space in the chaplain's office, away from the normal visitors' room,' he told me.

'Thank you,' I said gratefully. 'That will be much better for the children.'

'I'm afraid the only downside is it's a bit of a walk,' he said.

The place was like a rabbit warren of corridors and as one heavy metal door was opened, another was locked behind us. We walked deeper and deeper into the heart of the prison. We must have gone through a dozen doors and I started to feel really claustrophobic and fearful. I didn't know where I was, I didn't know any of these people and as I saw all these doors being locked behind us all I could think was, *What if there's a fire? How do we get out?*

It felt like there was no escape and it was horrible. I took big deep breaths and tried not to panic. I knew Evie and Elliot took their cues from me so I had to be calm, and looking at their big worried eyes I could see they were getting jittery.

'To get to the chaplain's office we have to go through the prison courtyard and then the visitors' room,' the officer explained.

The visitors' room was huge and crammed full of people. The noise of adults and children talking and shouting was deafening as it echoed off the walls around us. I was balancing Evie on my hip and holding Elliot's hand and I could feel them gripping on to me tighter and tighter as they got more and more tense.

'Nearly there now,' I soothed.

'It's just up here,' said the officer, leading us up a narrow flight of stairs above the chapel.

The chaplain's office looked like a storeroom with piles of boxes in the corner and stacks of black plastic chairs. The walls were painted a horrible brown colour and the carpet was a cheap royal blue needlecord. There was nothing homely or welcoming about it. Dean was already there, sitting on one of the black plastic chairs, flanked by two prison officers. There were three blue office chairs set out opposite him obviously for the kids and me.

'Here's Daddy,' I said in my most cheerful voice.

It had taken us three-quarters of an hour to get from the prison entrance to here. I was exhausted and I could see the children were overwhelmed. It was such a relief when I saw some crayons and paper on the floor.

'Oh look, there's some colouring,' I said. 'That's one of our favourites. Shall we all have a go?'

Evie finally agreed to be put down and release her vice-like grip on me, and we all sat down on the floor.

'Can I sit with them?' Dean asked one of the guards, and he gave him the nod to say he could get up.

Elliot happily sat with his dad on the floor while Evie plonked herself firmly on my lap.

'You're both getting so big,' said Dean. 'That's a pretty dress, Evie.'

Just like before, Evie refused to have anything to do with him and pressed herself against me. Elliot coloured in one of the pictures and Dean helped him.

'Come on, Evie, you have a go too,' I said. 'Show Daddy how good you are at colouring.'

While the children coloured, it was up to me to keep up the chit-chat. I knew we had to keep it light as I wanted their memories of the goodbye to be a positive one.

'Are we going to tell Daddy where we've been for lunch today?' I said. 'And what about your new shoes? We must show him those.'

But the children were more interested in doing their pictures and Dean didn't really have much to say to them.

It was a fifty-five-minute visit and, to be honest, I couldn't wait for it to be over. It was such an odd, unnatural situation and none of us could relax. I knew the kids were on edge and there were three security guards listening and watching our every move.

'Would it be OK to get the kids a drink?' I asked one of the prison officers.

He went off and ten minutes later came back with some beakers of orange squash. I handed them to Dean so that he could give them to the kids. Being in prison he had nothing to give Evie and Elliot so I knew even little gestures like that were important so that he could feel like their parent. Despite everything, these were still his children not mine, and I felt it was important for him, especially as it was for the last time.

I noticed there was a pile of picture books on a table in the corner of the room.

'Elliot, why don't you choose a book to look at with Daddy?' I said.

He went and got one and happily sat on his dad's lap. As Elliot flicked through the pages, Dean tenderly stroked the back of his neck and ruffled his fair hair.

'He's always had lovely soft hair,' he told me.

Dean had been remarkably calm and together up until now, but as he sat with Elliot, it was as if it suddenly hit him that this was the last time that he'd ever see his son. His eyes filled up with tears and, no matter how hard he tried, he couldn't stop himself from crying.

'That looks like a nice book, son,' he said, his voice quivering with emotion.

By now the tears were rolling down his face. He knew the magnitude of the situation and that after today he'd never ever see his children again. As a parent myself, I can't imagine what it feels like to have to say goodbye to your children for ever and, whatever Dean had done, I felt desperately sad for him.

He kept turning away and wiping his eyes to try and hide his tears from Elliot, but eventually he noticed. 'Oh, Daddy,' he said. 'Your face is all wet.'

'Here,' said one of the prison officers, handing him a tissue. Elliot reached out for it and I had to swallow a lump in my throat as I watched him tenderly pat his dad's cheeks dry.

I think saying goodbye to his kids in that manner was the biggest wake-up call Dean had ever had. All I could hope was that it would change his behaviour and make him turn his life around.

'Ten more minutes,' said one of the prison officers, pointing to the clock on the wall.

'Right, kids, we must take a nice photo of you and Daddy to put in your albums,' I told them. I knew it would be really important for them in the future to have a record of their last goodbye with Daddy.

I'd not been allowed to bring my own camera in so one of the officers said we could use the prison one. One of them even went and found a white tablecloth which he draped over a folded-up table-tennis table.

'It'll give the pictures a nicer backdrop,' he said, and I was touched they were trying to make the best of this horrible situation for the kids.

'Let's take a lovely photo of you and Daddy,' I told Evie, but when I tried to put her on his lap, she went crazy, kicking and screaming. She refused to go anywhere near him, so in the end I had to balance her on one of my knees and then lean out of the way so I wasn't in the picture.

'Say cheese,' said the prison officer, but no one was smiling.

Evie was scowling, Elliot stared straight ahead and Dean just looked shell-shocked, his eyes still wet with tears.

Our time was up and now we had to say our final goodbye.

'We have to go now, so do you want to go and give Daddy a hug bye-bye?' I told Elliot and Evie.

Although Elliot had been happy to sit with his dad, he looked a bit awkward and uncomfortable as he gave him a hug. Evie just buried her head underneath my tunic top and refused to go anywhere near him.

'Bye-bye, Daddy,' I said on behalf of the children, as neither of them was saying anything.

As we walked out, Dean looked desolate.

'I love you, son,' he called. 'And I love you too, Evie.'

As the door closed behind us, I heard him break down and start howling. It had obviously taken all his strength to hold it together while Evie and Elliot were there, but now they'd gone all his emotions came pouring out. It was hard to hear a grown man sobbing like that and once again I was struck by the overwhelming sadness of the situation.

'Will he be going straight back to the cells?' I asked the prison officer.

'Don't worry, we'll take him for a cup of tea and a chat with the chaplain first,' he said.

I was relieved that they weren't going to send him down in that state.

As we walked back through the prison and the endless locked doors, my heart felt heavy. I knew a little bit about Dean's background from Andrew and it was sad as it was a case of history repeating itself. He'd grown up in the care system after coming from a violent home, and he'd been physically abused in the children's homes that he'd lived in as a child. It didn't excuse his own violent behaviour but I could see that part of his distress was that his own children were now in the same care system that he'd been brought up in.

I felt sad for Elliot, too, as he'd just said goodbye to the one person that he had some emotional attachment to. I wasn't sure if he truly understood that this was for ever. He was used to Dad being in and out of his life but I'm not sure it had hit home that he'd just said goodbye for good.

When we finally emerged from the prison and walked back onto the street, it was such a relief. Evie and Elliot looked shell-shocked and I think I was too. On our way to the car we passed a little playground and the children immediately looked at me with pleading eyes.

'I promised you a park, so you can have a go,' I said.

After ten minutes on the swings and slides, the trauma of the last couple of hours seemed to have quickly been forgotten. The children seemed fine but I was a different matter. As I sat on a bench and watched them run around, I suddenly burst into tears. Going into a high-security prison had really got to me, as had the overwhelming sadness I felt about the whole situation.

But I was pleased that I'd pushed for the visit. It was an important step for the children and hopefully now they were saying goodbye to the past they could finally move on to the future and meet their for ever mummy and daddy. However, first we had to say goodbye to their mum, and I honestly didn't know how that was going to go.

EIGHTEEN

The Last Goodbye

The children ran up and down the aisles of the supermarket putting things into my basket. I looked through it, checking that we had everything on my list.

'Ginger star biscuits, tubes of coloured icing, sprinkles,' I said. 'Right, kids, I think we're done.'

As Evie and Elliot helped me load everything onto the conveyer belt at the checkout, I felt my mobile buzzing in my bag. It was Andrew.

'Hi, Maggie, just to let you know I've been round to collect Mum but she wasn't there,' he said.

'Well whatever happens we're coming to the contact centre to decorate the biscuits anyway, so we'll just play it by ear,' I said.

'OK, I'll keep you posted.'

As I hung up, I felt really annoyed and frustrated. Surely if you knew that it was the last time that you'd ever see your children you'd bother to turn up and say goodbye, wouldn't you?

Today Evie and Elliot were supposed to be seeing their mum Sheena for the last time. We'd arranged to do it at a contact centre where Andrew worked that we'd never been to before. I knew that we needed to take along some sort of activity with us to try and engage their mum and occupy the children. Then at least even if the goodbye itself didn't go well the kids could decorate the biscuits and take away something positive from it. Elliot especially needed some sort of distraction to even get him in the room with his mother in the first place.

As we got into the car in the supermarket car park I knew I had to prewarn the children that there was a possibility their mum might be there. I tried to be as casual as I could about it just in case she didn't show.

'We're going to go and see Andrew now and decorate the biscuits and I think Mummy might be coming too so we can give a biscuit to her.'

Evie didn't react at all, but at the mention of Mummy Elliot flinched.

'Why are we going to see Mummy?' he asked. 'You said we didn't have to see her again.'

'Remember when we were doing the puzzle how Andrew told you that you we needed to say bye-bye first?' I told him, and he nodded. 'Then once you've said goodbye you don't need to see Mummy ever again.'

I could see Elliot was already anxious about it as we pulled up outside the contact centre.

'Are you coming too, Maggie?' he asked warily as I got him out of the car.

'Yes, I'm going to be in the room with you and Evie,' I said.

Andrew had agreed I could stay with the children as I knew that was the only way Elliot would even go into the contact room. He'd only ever made it to one visit with his mum ever since they'd been taken into care, and that was a few minutes at the hospital entrance where he could still see me through the glass. I was determined this last contact with her would be as calm and as positive as possible.

'I think it's silly trying to force him to go in there on his own and just cause upset,' I'd said to Andrew. 'After all, it's the last time he's going to see her.'

'If being in the room stops Elliot getting hysterical and going into meltdown then I think you should do it,' he said.

We walked into the contact centre where Andrew was waiting for us.

'Any sign?' I said, but he shook his head. I could tell Elliot was on edge and he looked around nervously.

'Come on,' I said, taking his hand to reassure him. 'Let's get cracking with these biscuits.'

We went into the contact room which was small with a little table and chairs at one end and a sofa at the other. I was helping Evie and Elliot to take off their coats when the door opened and a woman shuffled in.

'Aah, here's Mummy,' said Andrew. 'Glad that you could get here in the end, Sheena.'

Sheena was small and pale with straggly brown hair and she reeked of stale alcohol and cigarettes. She was wearing ripped leggings and a tatty woollen jumper and she looked dirty and dishevelled, like she'd just got out of bed. She was carrying three carrier bags and I wondered if she'd brought some presents for the kids.

'Bloody buses,' she mumbled. 'Always late.'

She had a vacant, blank look in her eyes and she didn't say hello to the kids or even ask how they were. I didn't introduce myself as she didn't ask, and I didn't want to get too involved. The kids froze and moved nearer to me.

'The children have brought some biscuits to decorate so we thought you might like to sit and all do them together,' I said.

She shrugged.

'You can take one home with you if you want,' Elliot said.

'Nah,' she sighed with a look of disgust. 'Don't like ginger biscuits. They're disgusting.'

Then she turned her attention to Evie.

'My baby,' she said, throwing her arms around her and covering her with kisses. She tried to pick her up but Evie was having none of it and quickly wriggled away.

'All right, son,' she said to Elliot.

She didn't even try and touch him and he didn't say a word. I could see the minute that his mum had entered the room and made the comment about the biscuits Elliot had just cut himself off and shut down. I could physically see him withdraw into himself like he was saying, *You can't hurt me. I'm not really here.* It was his way of coping and protecting himself.

Andrew and I went and sat on the sofa in the corner, leaving Sheena and the children to decorate the biscuits together but what happened next beggared belief.

Sheena pulled up a chair, wedged herself in between the children then turned her chair around so that she was facing Evie but had her back to Elliot. I couldn't believe she was freezing him out like that.

'I missed you, baby,' she said, trying to pull Evie onto her knee.

Although Evie refused to sit on her lap she must have had some memory of her mum because she tolerated her over-the-top affection. I could see that Evie was like a little doll to Mum. Something cute to dress up and carry around, but that's as far as her parenting went.

Sheena focused all her attention on Evie and helped her to decorate a biscuit while Elliot just sat there. I couldn't bear to see him being ignored like that and I felt every bit of his rejection. That moment I saw with my own eyes how things must have been at home for him and it was heartbreaking. Seeing her turn her back on her son like that, any jot of sympathy that I'd ever felt for Sheena completely disappeared. She had no awareness whatsoever of what she had done to Elliot.

I pulled up a chair next to him and helped him to decorate his biscuit.

'What colours would you like to choose?' I asked him. 'Shall we put a few sprinkles on there too?'

The blank look was back in his eyes and, as I was talking, he reached out and stroked the side of my face. It was rare that he sought out physical contact so I could tell how much he must have needed it. I stroked his hair and held his hand for reassurance. My heart ached for him. I could feel him bristle every time he heard his mum talking to Evie.

Mum was busy telling Evie what to do. She had taken over the activity and had no interest in what Evie wanted.

Although Elliot hadn't seen his mum for months I could tell being in her presence still triggered unhappy memories for him. His body language said it all. He was sat stiff and rigid in his chair and he was so on edge. He kept pulling my sleeve up and looking at my watch even though he couldn't tell the time yet.

'What does the clock say, Maggie?' he asked me.

I knew he couldn't wait to get out of there. In a way I felt mean putting him through this ordeal but I knew he needed to do it. Hopefully one day it would bring him some closure and somewhere at the back of his mind he'd remember saying goodbye to Mummy. He needed this to get rid of his fears.

At one point Andrew went and got a digital camera.

'Right, everybody smile,' he said. 'I'm going to take a nice photo of you doing your biscuits with Mummy.'

I leaned out of the way so I wouldn't be in the picture. Sheena looked up and gave a false smile while Evie and Elliot just ignored the fact Andrew was taking a photo.

After about twenty minutes I could see Sheena was starting to fidget and rustle through her carrier bags, that obviously had nothing in them for the children.

'I'd best be off soon or I'll miss my bus,' she said.

'Don't worry about the bus,' Andrew told her. 'I'll give you a lift home so there's no rush.'

But she wasn't convinced and seemed determined to go.

'Before you leave, Sheena, I need to have a chat to you about a few things,' Andrew told her.

In the end, I decided there was no use prolonging this if she didn't want to be here. 'Right then, kids, is it time to go?'

'Yes!' said both of them eagerly, jumping up.

I helped them put on their coats and pack up the biscuits.

'Evie, would you like to have a cuddle bye-bye with Mummy?' I said, but she shook her head.

I didn't even ask Elliot as I knew what the answer would be.

'Well, let's say bye-bye to Mummy then,' I told them.

'Bye-bye,' said Evie, waving.

Elliot didn't say a word.

'Bye, kids,' she said and gave them a wave.

You would never guess it was the last time that she'd ever see her children again. There was no tears or emotion, no 'I love you' or 'have a good life'. In fact she'd had no interaction whatsoever with Elliot. She said goodbye so casually like she was just popping out to the shops for five minutes. As we walked out of the contact centre, I felt a real relief that that was over and done with.

In the car both children tucked into the ginger biscuit they'd decorated. As they munched away and chatted about the different-coloured icing they'd used, there was no mention whatsoever of Mummy. In fact they both seemed completely nonplussed about what had happened in there. Perhaps that was no bad thing, I just hoped that it would help Elliot to move on.

'That was nice seeing Mummy to say goodbye, wasn't it?' I said.

But neither of them said a word or mentioned Mummy again. That night, when the children were in bed, Andrew phoned.

'How do you think it went?' he asked.

'I thought it was strangely positive,' I told him. 'There was no tears or screaming and Elliot, bless him, got through it despite the complete lack of interest from his birth mother. He managed to stay in the room with her which was a first for him.'

'I know how blunt you are, Maggie. I half expected you to say something at one point,' he said.

'I really was fuming,' I told him.

But there would have been no point in kicking up a fuss. Their mother had no awareness whatsoever of the hurt she'd caused. Maybe losing her children like this would hit her in a few years. Maybe it wouldn't. I believed that she genuinely cared for Evie but she had no emotional connection to Elliot whatsoever.

A few days later, Andrew dropped round two copies of the photograph that he'd taken of them with their mum. We stuck Evie's copy into her memory book.

'Would you like a photo for your book, Elliot?' I asked.

He took the picture from me and studied it solemnly for ages.

'No, thank you,' he said, handing it back to me.

'Are you sure?' I asked.

'Very sure,' he said.

I smiled at his reply, because it was something my children said a lot that he'd obviously picked up on. After that he never ever mentioned his mother again.

As a foster carer I've learnt that you can't make people responsible for their behaviour. It wasn't my place to dish out blame or punishment. Whatever I felt, I knew it was important for the children to say goodbye because it ends things for them so they can move on and attach to new parents. I think it's important for the birth parent too. As a mum myself I couldn't think of anything more horrific than having to say goodbye to any of my kids. I don't even know if I could do it and I think it's a very brave thing for parents to do.

However, I was relieved that that chapter of their life was over for Evie and Elliot. Now I hoped they could finally let go of the past and start afresh.

NINETEEN

Blowing Out the Candles

Everyone waited in anticipation as I gave Tess the nod. She dimmed the kitchen lights while I quickly lit the candles.

'Right then. One, two, three . . .' I said, before launching into a rendition of 'Happy Birthday' hoping everyone else would join in singing to Evie and Elliot to drown out my tuneless wailing.

Evie buried her head shyly in my shoulder, uncharacteristically bashful at all the attention, however, Elliot had a huge smile on his face.

'Go on then,' I said, putting the huge chocolate cake down in front of them. 'Blow out your candles.'

There were four candles on one side for Elliot and three on the other for Evie. They'd both told me they'd never had a birthday cake before so I'd made the biggest gooiest creation possible and sprinkled the top with Smarties. There had been enough birthdays in this house since they'd arrived seven months ago to know what to do and they were both beaming with pride as they blew out their candles.

Handily, Evie and Elliot's birthdays were four days apart so I'd organised a joint party on the Sunday that fell in between them. I'd done a traditional tea party and we played pass the parcel and pin the tail on the donkey. It was the first time in their lives they'd ever had a party and they'd loved every minute of it. I'd invited my friends Wendy, Vicky and Anne over with their foster children and Elliot's friend Ethan from preschool.

Evie adored her present – a pink Silver Cross doll's pram that I'd found on eBay – and I'd knitted her a matching patchwork blanket to go over her Baby Annabell doll. But I think what she loved most were the five Cinderella helium balloons tied to the handles. Elliot had got a Playmobil zoo which he loved.

Again I wanted to spoil them as I knew their birthdays had never been celebrated in the past. They'd led a life where there had been no cakes or parties or presents, so I wanted to share those traditions with them and in a way start their childhood. Birthdays made children feel important and special and I wanted Evie and Elliot to experience that. It had been a lovely day with family and friends and thankfully they'd enjoyed every minute of it. They were genuinely happy and, unlike at Christmas, they weren't puzzled or bemused by it. They understood about presents now and so there was a real build-up of excitement around their birthdays. It was lovely just to see them enjoying being children.

Now that Evie and Elliot had said their goodbyes to their biological parents we were slowly going to introduce the idea of adoption to them.

'I think it would be beneficial for them to have some play therapy,' suggested Andrew at one of our planning meetings.

'I think it would be a good way for them to work through saying goodbye to their biological parents and to help them understand about families.'

Simon and I both liked the idea, but I felt that in order for the therapy to work it needed to be at my house.

'If you want the children to go into the sessions on their own then it needs to be here,' I said. 'The kids have settled into preschool well but they're still not confident going off with a stranger without me. It just won't happen if it's in an office somewhere. They need to feel comfortable and relaxed in order for them to open up.'

I'd seen play therapy work well in the past. It was a good way for younger children to express their fears and emotions that they sometimes couldn't verbalise themselves. Watching the way children played also often brought out some of their deep-rooted fears and worries, and I thought Evie and Elliot could benefit from that.

Before the sessions started, the therapist Anna came round to my house for a meeting with Andrew, Simon and I. As soon as I met her I liked her and I knew the children would respond well to her. She was very tall with a short blonde bob, and she had a gentle manner and a calm, soft voice.

'We'll hold the first six sessions in Maggie's front room and once we feel the children have got to know Anna and are a bit more relaxed then we can look at transferring them to an office,' said Andrew.

'I'll come round for a cup of tea first so the children see me with you,' said Anna. 'I think if Elliot and Evie see you chatting to me and that you're happy and comfortable with me then that gives them permission to talk.'

A few days later, when the children were at preschool, Anna came round to choose some toys that she could use in their sessions.

'I'll bring some with me but I think it's good to have some toys they already know there too to give them some familiarity,' she said.

Together we selected some crayons and little animal figures, a magic wand and some musical toys.

'Elliot loves cars so it would be good to have some of those,' I said. 'And the different-coloured threading buttons are a favourite of his too.'

I'd ordered some new toys too that I knew would intrigue them and make them want to play and explore. There were some new bendy figures for the doll's house, some hand puppets and some glittery Play-Doh that I knew Evie would absolutely love. I put them all in a special box decorated with little elephants. Anna and I agreed I'd put it in the front room each time they had a session and then move it to the cupboard under the stairs, so it only came out for therapy.

Before Anna's first visit I explained to Evie and Elliot what was happening.

'A lady's coming round to talk to me today and then she's going to talk to you,' I said gently. 'And she's going to bring some special toys with her for you to play with. Won't that be fun?'

They seemed fine with the idea, but when she arrived they watched her warily. As planned, I had a cup of tea with her in the kitchen while the children played next to us. I wanted them to see that I liked her and that I thought she was safe person to have in the house.

After a while Anna said, 'Oh, Maggie I've brought some new

toys round that I thought you might like. Do you want to come and have a look at them?'

'Ooh, yes please,' I said, trying to sound convincing. 'That sounds very exciting.'

Anna and I went into the front room and predictably at the promise of new and exciting toys, Evie and Elliot followed. They were soon engrossed in going through what was in the mysterious box with Anna. As they looked at the toys, she tried to explain to them why she was there.

'My job is to play with children like you who don't live with their mummies and daddies,' she said gently. 'Sometimes children feel angry, upset or muddled about that, so we play about these feelings.'

I'm not sure they really understood but they were keen to get their hands on the toys. I stayed with them for about ten minutes then I made my excuses.

'I've got to go back to the kitchen and do my cooking now but I'll leave the door open so you can hear me in there.'

I wanted the sessions to be as relaxed as possible and I never stopped the children from running in and out of the kitchen to show me something or ask me a question. I didn't want to put pressure on them to stay in the room or keep away from me as I knew that would have just made them clam up and be reluctant to go with Anna.

That first forty-five-minute session the children just played with Anna, exploring the contents of the box. That needed to happen first to reassure them that she was a nice, safe person and they'd both be fine with her.

The following week Evie was asleep when Anna arrived so Elliot had his session first.

'Would you like to come and see my toys again?' she asked.

Elliot shrugged and by the look on his face I could see that he was thinking, *Why are they making me do this?* He went with Anna although I could see he was very unsure and wary. He kept coming into the kitchen telling me that he needed a wee.

'Well, you know where the toilet is and you can go yourself,' I told him.

I knew it was just a way of avoiding being in the room with Anna.

'How did that go?' I asked her afterwards.

'Well, he was very cautious and hesitant and he needed a lot of reassurance,' she said. 'It's almost like he felt embarrassed or wouldn't allow himself to play in front of me, and when he did it was very repetitive.

'When I asked him about his parents he said that his daddy lived in a building and that Mummy lived with Daddy.'

Poor little thing. He was obviously still very confused about his biological parents and what had happened.

Evie had woken up from her nap by now and she was very shy and reluctant to go with Anna at first so we used the enticement of the new glittery Play-Doh.

'If you want to play with this then you'll have to go into the front room and play as we don't want to get glitter in the cooking, do we?' I told her.

So she went with Anna but she kept running back into the kitchen.

'Mummy, will you come and look at the toys with me?'

'No, I'm afraid I'm busy in the kitchen but Anna will. I'll be in here, though,' I told her.

As the session went on, I could tell that she was getting into it more and I could hear her laughing and chatting. Evie seemed a lot more receptive to it than Elliot had been.

'She was very withdrawn at first and she made me show her what was in the box rather than her having a look herself,' said Anna afterwards. 'But once she got into it and felt more comfortable she was very chatty. She has a really good imagination.'

'She has,' I said proudly. 'She's come on so much.'

The therapy seemed to have affected Elliot the most. After Anna left, he was terribly grumpy and I couldn't help but wonder if talking about his biological parents again had upset him. At teatime nothing was right and I couldn't do anything to please him.

'I don't want this cup,' he complained. 'And I don't like that plate.'

'What cup and plate would you like then, lovey?' I asked.

In the bath that night he wasn't happy about the toys or the book I read him before bed. All I could do was give him choices so he felt like he had some sense of control back. I think he'd start to cotton on to the fact that things were changing and the next part of his life was happening, and he was unsure and scared about the future.

Anna came the following week and there was one thing in particular that I was very keen for her to do with the children, to make sure they'd got the idea of saying goodbye to their biological parents.

'It's something I read in an American book and I thought Evie and Elliot might really like it,' I told her.

The idea was the children would bring two cakes into the therapy room and Anna would light a candle on each of their cakes. Then she would say: 'Say goodbye to your old mummy and daddy' and they'd both blow the candle out. Then they'd light a new candle on each of their cakes that represented a new mummy and daddy. I thought it was a really good, simple way of drawing a line over their past and helping them move forward. Even if they didn't get it or were reluctant to do it, the worst that could happen was they got a cake each to eat.

'Well I'm willing to try it if you think it might help,' Anna told me.

The morning before Anna was due to come for a session, Evie and Elliot helped me bake some cakes. Elliot wanted green icing on his and Evie wanted pink on hers.

'Now Anna wants you to take a cake each and these candles into the front room with her because she's going to do something very special with you,' I told them when she arrived.

They ran in there happily – they didn't need any encouragement when it came to eating cake. Five minutes later Elliot came running into the kitchen.

'Maggie,' he said, holding out his hand to me. 'Come quickly.'

'What is it?' I asked him. 'What's wrong?'

'I want you to come and help me blow goodbye to Mummy.'

Bless him, I think it was really important to him that I was there. He wanted me to know that his mummy really had gone, and it was almost as if if I was there to see it then it must be true. Evie, meanwhile, didn't have a clue. She was more concerned that candle wax was going to drip on her pink icing and she couldn't wait to blow it out so she could tuck in.

'Eat cake now,' she said, jumping up and down with glee.

I could see that it was a significant moment for Elliot and it meant something to him. He paused for a moment, closed his eyes then blew his flame out.

'All gone,' he sighed.

I think it was extra reassurance for him that he really didn't have to see his mummy or live with her again.

After three sessions we decided to do what we'd originally planned and move the therapy sessions to an office.

'What about our agency offices?' suggested Simon. 'You could do them in the contact room there.'

'That's a good idea,' I replied.

The children had been there with me many times for coffee mornings or to pop in and see Simon. They knew the building and they'd been in that room before – it was small and cosy with a settee and table in it. I knew they'd be more comfortable there than at Social Services.

Changing venue was also going to be a bit of a test. Both Simon, Andrew and I were keen to see how the children would cope. Yes, there had been so much progress and so many positive changes, but I was cautious that the adoption didn't happen too quickly as I still felt there was a long way to go before the children were truly ready.

'I think they can cope better but I think they're still incredibly fearful of change,' I said.

It was a bit like the time I'd tried to pop out to the shops when Simon offered to look after the kids when they'd first arrived. I could tell social workers what the kids were like but it was also useful if they could see it for themselves. They'd seen Evie and Elliot happy and relaxed at my house and had decided that they were better and had moved on. But it was important for them to realise that, even in my house with me there, it had still taken a huge effort for them to do the therapy with Anna.

I hoped the children could cope with seeing Anna at the new venue, but if they didn't it was useful that other people could witness it. If the children's anxiety and fear and inability to cope with change was documented in a report it was proof for me that the adoption process needed to slow down and go at their pace.

I broke the news to the children that morning.

'You're not going to go to preschool today,' I told them. 'Instead of Anna coming here to play you're going to play with her at Simon's office.'

Neither Elliot nor Evie were happy about that.

'Why?' said Elliot. 'Why can't she come here?'

'Because I can't have people in my front room today,' I said.

'No,' wailed Evie. 'I don't want to go.'

'Why do we have to go there?' said Elliot.

I felt slightly mean doing it to them but I knew in the long run it was for their own benefit. Both of them looked very anxious and unsure.

'I want my blanket,' wailed Evie.

'What blanket?' I asked, as she'd never left the house with a blanket before.

'The one on my bed,' she said.

So I ran upstairs and got her the fleecy blanket from the end of her bed. I could see Elliot was nervous too so I gave him a teddy to try and reassure him.

'Elliot, can you take this teddy bear and look after it for me because the bear needs to come back home after your play session?'

He just nodded and I could tell that he was trying not to cry.

'Elliot, I promise you your new mummy and daddy won't be there if that's what you're worried about. It's just Anna and the toys.'

He looked so bewildered and scared and I didn't know what was going through his little mind. I drove the children to the agency offices and Elliot waited with Simon while I took Evie into the contact room.

'Look, it's Anna,' I said, but she clung onto me like a limpet.

'Mummy come too,' she mumbled. 'Mummy stay.'

I didn't want to have to pull Evie off me and leave her in the room and if I did then I knew she was going to get hysterical and then it would be game over. There would definitely be no therapy session.

I looked at Anna and she nodded.

'OK,' I said. 'I'll stay.'

Evie insisted on sitting on my knee although I didn't get involved in the actual playing.

'Now today we're going to play with a family of animals,' Anna told her.

Evie happily played with the four little models. I watched as she got the tiger and started snapping at the other three animals and then pushed them to the floor.

'Oh dear, what's happened?' asked Anna.

'The tiger's bit all the other animals in his family,' she said.

'And what's happened to them?'

'That one's dead and those two have to go to hospital to get made better,' she said matter-of-factly.

Every time Evie played with the animals it was always the same scenario.

Her play was all about families where one hurt the others. Sometimes they got better and other times they didn't recover. They also got the puppets out and Anna wrote a sticky label for each one 'Mummy', 'Daddy', 'Evie' and 'Elliot' and stuck them onto the puppets' heads. Then Anna acted out little scenes guided by Evie. It was fascinating to watch. Whenever Evie was being the mummy puppet she would just cry and if she was the daddy she made a terrifying roaring noise.

'Where are your mummy and daddy, Evie?' Anna asked.

'Daddy's at work and Mummy's poorly,' she said.

Afterwards I had a word with Anna while Evie slumped on the settee looking exhausted.

'I think it's clear that Evie remembers a lot more of the domestic violence than we'd realised,' she said. 'But by acting it out through play like this hopefully it will help her put those memories to bed.'

I hoped she was right. Afterwards Evie was tired and clingy, and while Elliot had his session she curled up in my arms and fell asleep.

Elliot looked terrified but I was so proud of him when he agreed to go into the session with Anna on his own.

'How was it?' I asked her afterwards.

'He was completely overwhelmed by anxiety,' she said.

She described how he'd been hyper-vigilant – constantly checking out every noise he heard and who was around, and he'd had endless trips to the toilet.

'Has he got a tummy bug?' she asked, but I shook my head.

'I think it's just an avoidance tactic he uses when he's feeling anxious,' I said.

She described how Elliot had played with the puppets.

'Anything involving him and Mummy and he froze,' she said. 'The puppets literally didn't move and his play came to a complete standstill. It was as if he'd just closed down completely.'

The therapy carried on over the next few weeks but the children still struggled to cope with the change in venue.

'Unfortunately it's as I expected,' I told Simon. 'They've still got a lot of deep-seated anxiety and insecurity.'

They were comfortable and happy with Anna in my house but they couldn't transfer that attachment.

'It proves to me that they wouldn't be able to transfer their attachment to their adopters,' I said.

'What do you think needs to happen then?' he asked.

'I hope it's just a matter of time,' I said. 'In time that will happen and they'll learn to transfer their attachment. They did it with preschool. It might be an age-related thing and they just haven't got that skill yet.

'If we try and push through an adoption now, it will fail,' I said. 'We need to take it really slowly.'

I knew we needed to discuss our fears with Andrew too. Thankfully Anna's reports on the children backed up my feelings.

Evie is a lively little girl but she was initially reluctant to engage. She needs a safe environment and a clear routine – she needs to be carefully prepared for any changes in her life to minimise her anxiety. To her, adults aren't trustworthy or reliable and her anxiety or fear could be triggered by small changes to her routine like a visitor to the house or an unfamiliar food being offered to her.

Elliot is an anxious little boy and very unsure of the world he lives in. Like his sister, he doesn't trust adults or feel safe. He was sad, anxious and confused about his parents and where they were. His memories of the past trouble him deeply.

It was all true but it still made sad reading. The children had a long way to go. Hopefully their fear would be replaced one day by joy. But until then there was no way they were ready for adoption.

TWENTY

Progress and Change

As spring passed and we headed towards the summer, the children slowly made more progress. Meanwhile, in the background, social workers began to look at finding them permanent parents.

It sounds silly but one of the ways that I knew the children were moving forward was by looking at their eyes. After the first few weeks with me Evie and Elliot had put on weight and their cheeks had filled out, but there was still an awful blankness to their faces. I find that kids who don't have attachment to people have no expression. When you look at them it's like looking into nothing and you can physically see the emotional neglect. So you can give them clean sheets, hot meals and the reliability of a routine, however, unless you can actually get into their brains and engage with them emotionally then you don't have any real or lasting effect. I know that I've truly reached them when their eyes start to shine.

Evie's eyes had quickly changed. However, nine months on, Elliot's sparkle was taking a long time to come. I was confident that he was slowly getting there. Starting preschool had definitely brought about a change in him. It had given him confidence and encouraged his imagination. I could see it in the way that he played. I watched him one morning in the kitchen as he played Duplo with Evie. In the past, he'd have just sat there and there would have been no conversation between them. Eventually Evie might have asked, 'Is that a crocodile, Elliot?' and he would have responded with a one-word 'yes' or 'no' answer. This particular morning, as I loaded up the dishwasher, I was thrilled to hear him chatting away to his sister.

'What you making, El?'

'A crocodile,' he said. 'I think I'll give it sharp teeth.'

'That's scary,' said Evie.

'And a long nose so it can go snap snap,' he replied, teasing her by making a snapping motion near her head.

I loved hearing him talk through his ideas and be engaged and involved in his play. It was wonderful seeing him use his imagination and decide what he wanted to build rather than put a few bricks together and then decide what it looked like.

Going to preschool had opened up their little world and allowed them to have experiences independently of me and each other, and they enjoyed telling me about it. Like any typical nursery-age child, Elliot came home each day with armfuls of paintings and blobs of grey clay that he'd made that day. He'd tell me what he'd drawn or painted and I'd praise him. One afternoon he came home with a huge painting that looked like a series of swirls.

'It's a pirate ship, Maggie,' he said proudly.

'It's lovely,' I said. 'It's so clever how you've used all those colours to make it so bright and cheerful and I love the flag on the top.'

'No, that's a parrot,' he said.

'Silly me, what a lovely parrot,' I told him.

'Do you think you could put it up on the kitchen wall?' he asked.

I was taken aback but I tried not to show it.

'Of course I can,' I said. 'I'll give it pride of place so we can all see it when we're sat around the table having our dinner.'

It was just a little thing but it showed me how far Elliot had come. He'd always made me put his artwork into the cupboard as if he was ashamed of it. This was the first time that he seemed proud of his work. Soon my kitchen walls were full of his pictures and as my display grew, so did his confidence and self-esteem.

Elliot also took it upon himself to become what we called the house 'pack-up monitor'. Every afternoon he'd get a little whiteboard and go round all of the other kids and ask them what they wanted in their packed lunch the next day. He'd write it down and then come to me and tell me. Nobody could understand a word that he'd written but he must have done because he never got it wrong.

'Tess wants a ham sandwich, Sam wants a cheese and Pete wants a tuna,' he'd tell me. 'And Evie and me will have ham too.'

He and Evie didn't even need a pack-up as they came home from preschool for lunch but I'd do them one anyway and leave it in the kitchen for when they got back, so they didn't feel left out. Then he'd tell me what kind of fruit everyone wanted and also what snack they'd like that day. For him to do that off his own bat showed me lots of things. It showed me that he was confident enough to take the initiative and ask everyone what they wanted and it also showed me that he was aware that everyone had different needs and likes.

Every day Elliot surprised me. One weekend I met up with my friend Anne and we took all the children to a soft play centre. When she came back to my house afterwards neither of us could be bothered cooking.

'Shall I nip to Maccy D's and bring us all a burger home for tea?' she said, grabbing her car keys.

'Great idea,' I replied.

Her two foster children Jamie and Nick wanted to go with her and they were pulling their shoes on when Elliot came running into the kitchen.

'Please can I come too?' he asked Anne.

'Of course you can, love,' she said.

As he went to get his coat and shoes on, I was gobsmacked. It was the first time that he'd willingly gone off anywhere without me. I didn't say anything as I didn't want to ruin the moment but Anne and I both looked at each other and smiled as he followed the boys out of the door without even a backwards glance. We both knew what a huge moment it was for Elliot and just showed how much he'd changed from the little boy who a few months ago wouldn't even let me go to the toilet on my own.

I'd worked so hard on making Elliot feel confident and secure with me, however, I knew the adoption process was really going to test that to the limits. Now he and Evie had said goodbye to their birth parents and a little bit of time had elapsed, I needed to start getting them used to the idea of finding them a new mummy and daddy.

'You know how much they're terrified of change so anything we do needs to be very gentle and gradual,' I told Andrew.

'Why don't you start with a few books about adoption,' he suggested. 'What about reading Dennis Duckling to them?'

Dennis Duckling was all about a duck who has to leave his mum and dad because they can't look after him so he goes to live on a different pond where he's cared for by other ducks.

I laughed and shook my head.

'There's no way I'm reading them that.' I smiled. 'You know how literally those kids take everything. They really will think they're going to be adopted by ducks not human beings!'

I'd got a couple of more simple, straightforward books about families and adoption that I'd used in the past and read one to them every few nights. I wanted to get them used to the idea that families come in all different forms. Some children I'd looked after in the past had been adopted by two mummies or two daddies so I had books that explored all sorts of different family units. Being a single mum, they knew there was no daddy around in our house so they were already familiar with that scenario. We live in a changing world and it was important for Evie and Elliot to realise that it was love, togetherness and stability that were important, not what gender your parents were.

The adoption process can take months but while Andrew was circulating the children's details to social workers to see if any potential adopters might be interested in Evie and Elliot, I had to start talking about the idea with them.

'Shall we find you a new mummy and daddy?' I said to them one day. 'We'll get Andrew to have a really good look to see who's out there and find you someone nice.'

They were quite resistant to it at first.

'*You're* my mummy,' said Evie.

'Oh, I'm Mummy Maggie but we're going to find you a lovely new mummy,' I told her.

I can't pretend that it's not hard when foster children go for adoption. It's a bittersweet moment for me but part of being a good foster parent is learning how to let go, and it's a skill that I've learnt over time. As much as we loved Evie and Elliot and wanted to keep them, I knew we would always have been a substitute family for them and they deserved their own parents. They needed the security of having someone special just for them.

Both Evie and Elliot were very uncertain about having a new mummy and daddy. Elliot in particular had a lot of worries but I tried to reassure him.

'Will we still have breakfast, lunch and dinner if we get a new mummy and daddy?'

'Of course you will,' I said.

'And can we take our toys?' asked Evie.

'Yes, you can take all your things to your new mummy and daddy's house,' I said.

'How will they know how warm we like our bath?' Elliot piped up.

'Because before you go and live in your new house your new mummy and daddy will come and give you a bath here and we'll show them exactly what temperature you like it.'

But Elliot didn't look convinced.

'Will we still see you?' he asked.

Eventually it was up to the adopters whether they wanted to keep in touch with me or not but there was always something in the plan that stated when the children would see me. It was a way of reassuring them that I still cared about them and hadn't just disappeared out of their lives.

'Yes, of course I'm going to see you, and before you leave here I'll make sure that you know exactly when that's going to be.'

'Will you miss us?' said Elliot sadly.

'How can I miss you, silly, when I'm going to see you?' I told him.

Of course I was going to miss them terribly but I knew it wouldn't help them let go and move on if I was weeping and wailing every day about how much we were going to miss them and how upset I was going to be when they left. No matter what I felt inside, I knew I had to keep it light, upbeat and positive in front of the kids.

I tried to make it fun too. I took them to Ikea and bought them a cardboard playhouse each.

'Pretend this is your new house and decorate it with all the colours that you'd like,' I told them.

Elliot's was very realistic and he spent ages painting bricks on it and a grey roof. Evie's was a riot of colour with a green roof and flowers, ribbons and pom-poms all over it.

'That's not a proper house,' Elliot told her.

But Evie loved it and she insisted on sitting in there every day and eating her sandwiches.

Andrew was really good at coming up with creative ways to talk about adoption and families with the kids. He came round one day and spent ages playing with the doll's house with them. They moved the figures around the house and put the baby to bed.

'What sort of bedroom would you like in your new house with your new mummy and daddy, Evie?' he asked.

'I'd like a pink room with a Cinderella bed,' she said.

'What about you, Elliot?'

'A blue bedroom with lots of planets in it,' he said as he was really fascinated by space.

'Is there anything else you'd like to have in your new house?' he asked.

'A trampoline in the garden and a dog,' said Elliot with a grin on his face.

'Yeah, a trampoline,' said Evie.

'Well, I'll see what I can do,' Andrew told them.

They both had their own fears. For Elliot it was fear of what a mum was, so I tried to tap into his desire for a daddy as that was something we didn't have in our house.

'Wouldn't it be nice to have a daddy to mend our bikes when they're broken because I have to get Mark across the road to do it.' I sighed when the chain came off Elliot's bike. 'It would be great to have a daddy around who could fix things.'

Evie wasn't keen on the idea of daddies, so for her I focused on her new mummy.

'What would you like your new mummy to be like?' I asked Evie.

'Someone who does cooking and sewing,' she said.

'A bit like Maggie?' Tess piped up and Evie nodded.

I wasn't worried that Evie wouldn't attach to her new foster mum. She'd attached to me and in my mind that proved she could transfer her attachment.

Every opportunity I had I talked about their new mummy and daddy so it became part of our everyday conversation. When I made spaghetti bolognaise one night I said to Elliot, 'I'm going to have to write this recipe down so your new mummy knows it's your favourite.'

When we went out shopping and I'd see clothes that I knew they'd like in a bigger size I'd show Evie and Elliot.

'Ooh look, shall I buy this and you can take it with you to your new mummy and daddy's house?'

The children didn't say much but I hoped it was all sinking in. I had to laugh one day as Elliot got cross with me after we'd had another argument about socks.

'I don't like you any more,' he said grumpily. 'When's my new mummy coming?'

I couldn't help but smile to myself as this showed me that he had been taking in and absorbing everything that I'd said.

Evie too had started to recognise family units and mummies and daddies. We had a day out with my friend Anne and her husband Bob and I could see her watching them like a hawk all day.

'Where's our daddy?' she asked me that night. 'Why don't we have a daddy like Bob?'

'I'm too busy looking after children to find a daddy,' I joked.

That night we were all sat watching *X Factor*. The kids all knew that I was a huge fan of Simon Cowell and that I always agreed with him. Halfway through the programme Evie pointed to the TV and said excitedly, 'That's our daddy!'

From then on, it became a standing joke in our house that I was going to marry Simon Cowell and he was going to live with us and be our 'daddy'. I was sure Evie knew that I would never really marry Simon Cowell because he was a man off the telly but she knew he was someone that I liked who made me laugh and smile and she'd recognised that's what daddies did.

'Daddy's on the telly!' she'd shout when *X Factor* was on.

I had to laugh to myself. We were due a new adoption worker; Lord knows what they were going to make of me and my fake TV 'husband' and Evie thinking that Simon Cowell was her daddy!

TWENTY-ONE

A Plea

Evie and Elliot's lives were suddenly filled with talk of their new mummy and daddy but the tricky thing was none of us knew how long it was going to take to find them these new parents. Then one day Andrew called with an update.

'Good news,' he said. 'There's a couple who are interested in Evie and Elliot.'

He couldn't tell me any more about them other than they lived half an hour away and didn't have any children of their own.

'I'm going round to meet them with their adoption worker and answer any questions they might have about the kids,' he told me.

'Good luck,' I told him.

I never allowed myself to get excited until much further down the line. I wasn't going to invest in these people until I knew they were going to invest in the kids. This part of the adoption process was just a waiting game and all I could do was cross my fingers. Of course I couldn't say a word about this to Evie and Elliot either, just in case the couple changed their minds and decided they didn't want to take it any further.

When Andrew called again a few days later it all sounded very positive.

'They're keen to go ahead and say they definitely want the kids,' he told me. 'They were offered two sets of children and they chose Evie and Elliot. They really feel like they'd fit in well with their family.'

Their names were Charlotte and Richard and they'd been married for ten years and had been through several failed attempts at IVF before deciding to go down the adoption route.

'Maggie, I've got a really good feeling about them,' he said. 'I think you're going to like them.'

They certainly sounded perfect. Richard was a steelworker and Charlotte worked in a florist's. He liked DIY, Charlotte was very crafty and enjoyed knitting and sewing, and they had a dog.

'Elliot is going to love that.' I smiled.

The next step was for myself, Andrew and Simon to meet Charlotte and Richard's adoption worker, Karen, so I could talk to her about the children and their needs. We all met up at my house a few days later.

'This is Karen,' said Andrew, introducing me to a large, sour-faced woman in her fifties.

I didn't warm to her at all and within the first few minutes of meeting her the hairs on the back of my neck were standing on end. The purpose of the meeting was for me to talk to her about the children and where they were at, but she just wanted to rush through everything and I didn't feel like she was listening to me.

'Elliot's anxiety levels are still very high,' I said, describing how he was when he first came to me. 'We couldn't leave the house for the first few months because of his screaming. He's a lot better but I don't think he's quite there yet.'

'Well it's only natural for children to be anxious about being adopted,' she said.

'But I think it's important that we work with that anxiety and slow everything right down,' I told her.

'I think it's important that we get Elliot to move on,' she said brusquely.

My hackles were really starting to rise now. I wanted her to know that although Elliot had come a long way, I wanted to have a little bit more time with him before he was adopted as I didn't feel that he was ready.

'He really struggles with attachment,' I said.

'Well that's good then as it means he'll move on more easily,' she replied, scribbling something down in her notepad.

I gave Simon a look and he knew exactly what I was thinking. This woman just didn't get it. She wasn't looking at Evie and Elliot as individuals and working out what their needs were. For her it was more about getting the job done as quickly as possible and ticking that box, just like Jenny had done. I knew I had to spell it out to her in black and white.

'Look, Karen,' I said. 'No matter how ideal or lovely your couple is, if this adoption is rushed through in a matter of weeks then it will fail. Elliot is just not ready and I need a little bit more time with him.'

But I knew Karen wasn't listening to me. She seemed more concerned by the fact that Evie referred to me as 'Mummy'.

'Well, we'll definitely have to put a stop to this mummy business before the adoption,' she said.

'I honestly don't think we need to,' I told her. 'I think it will resolve itself naturally when Evie meets her new mummy. I think it's a positive thing as it proves to me that Evie can attach to people. She successfully transferred her attachment to me so it means she can do it again.'

I knew Simon was on my side but as the children's social worker, it was Andrew that I needed to convince. He phoned me later that day.

'I'm guessing that you weren't exactly enamoured by Karen,' he said.

'Can you see why?' I replied.

'Look, Maggie, between you and I, Karen thinks the problem is that you're too attached to the children and you're not ready to let them go. That's why you're asking for more time.'

I was incensed. 'With respect, Andrew, I've done this enough times over twenty years to know how to let go,' I said.

'Oh, I know that,' he said. 'I told her that it's not about you. It's about the children being ready, and in your opinion Evie and Elliot are not ready.'

I just hoped that he agreed with me. When he came round one day I had a chat with him about it.

'It's tricky, Maggie, as I'm being pulled both ways,' he said. 'I've got you in one ear and Karen in the other.'

I knew I could tell him my concerns until I was blue in the face but what I really needed to do was show him.

'I tell you what,' I said. 'The children know you and they've built up a good relationship with you, haven't they? You're someone familiar to them?'

'Yes, I like to think so,' he said.

'Well, you go into the kitchen now and ask Evie and Elliot if they'd like to go for a little walk with you.' I told him. 'They can take their jars and their clipboards and it's a familiar route.'

I knew that if they refused point-blank to go with him then it would help prove my point. Andrew took up my suggestion and asked the kids if they'd like to go on a jar walk with him.

'No thanks,' said Elliot straight away.

'No, no,' said Evie, shaking her head.

I even tried to encourage them to go.

'Andrew would love to go for a little walk with you,' I said. 'It will be fun and I've got your special jars ready and a list of things to find.'

'Is Maggie coming too?' Elliot asked Andrew.

'Not today,' he said. 'But I'll be with you and we'll be back home in ten minutes.'

But neither Evie nor Elliot would entertain the idea and, although they weren't upset, they looked very anxious at his suggestion.

'You see,' I told Andrew. 'If they won't even go with someone they know and feel comfortable with, then what hope have new adoptive parents got?'

Sometimes people had to see it to understand it and I hoped it was enough to make Andrew understand my concerns.

'Your problem, Maggie, is that you make things look too easy.' He smiled.

But I just knew the children needed that little bit more continuity and security so that when things did change, they could cope. They needed to know that although things do change it will be OK and sometimes the biggest healer of all was time.

They needed time to fill their heads with normal, everyday things and swap their fear for enjoyment.

A few weeks later Richard and Charlotte, Evie and Elliot's prospective adoptive parents, went to what was called a matching panel. This was where a group of professionals had information about them and about Evie and Elliot and they decided whether they thought they were a good match for the children.

Andrew passed on the good news that the panel had decided that Charlotte and Richard were suitable adopters for the children and they'd given them the green light.

'Karen would like to come round and meet Evie and Elliot now the adoption's going ahead,' Andrew told me.

I wasn't relishing the thought of seeing Karen again, but I explained to the kids what was happening. I still couldn't tell them anything about Richard and Charlotte as we wouldn't do that until right before they were introduced to the children.

'A lady called Karen is going to come round and see us today,' I told them. 'She's going to help Andrew look for a new mummy and daddy for you and she wants to come and meet you first.'

I could tell the kids were as bemused by Karen as I was. She put on a high-pitched baby voice when she was speaking to them and they gave me a look as if to say, *Who is this woman?*

'Oh, here they are,' she squeaked as she walked into the kitchen where they were playing.

'Ooh, Evie, you look gorgeous in that priddy dwess and shoes,' she cooed. 'Aren't you lovely? And little Elliot, such a handsome ikkle fella.'

Evie just stared at Karen and I could tell she didn't know what to make of this over-the-top woman.

'Oh, yes, you do like that dress, don't you, Evie. It's one of your favourites,' I said, trying to reassure her.

Elliot was very wary of her and he and Evie joined me on the floor to do a puzzle. Thankfully Karen didn't get down on the floor with us so she just sat on the settee and watched. Afterwards we had a chat in the front room.

'Now I'd like to come round with Andrew at some point and do a DVD of the children to show Richard and Charlotte,' she said.

'That's not a problem,' I told her.

It was standard practice to do a little film for the adopters once they'd been approved by the panel. They couldn't meet the children just yet so a DVD gave them more of a sense of the kids and a chance to see them in action and hear their voices, as up until now all they would have seen were photographs.

The following week Andrew and Karen came round with a camcorder. Andrew did the filming while Karen just seemed to whip Evie and Elliot up into a frenzy. She had them playing games and running around and doing peekaboo for the camera under a blanket. It was all a bit hyper for my liking and it wasn't a true reflection of how the kids were at all. I couldn't bear to watch so I made my excuses and went to the kitchen to make a cup of tea. After a while Elliot sneaked out to join me.

'I don't want to do that camera thing any more,' he said.

'Why don't you come back into the front room with me and we'll do a jigsaw instead?' I suggested.

A few weeks after the matching panel in July, a meeting was organised to decide what the plan for the adoption was.

Sometimes adoptions could happen in a matter of weeks after the panel and this was an important meeting for me as I wanted to convince everyone that in Elliot and Evie's case this wasn't a good idea. I wanted to delay things for a few months as I was still concerned that Elliot wasn't quite ready.

It was a big, important meeting. Simon would be there as well as Andrew, Karen, Karen's boss and Anna the play therapist, who I was hoping would back up my point about the children's anxiety levels. It was also the first time that I was going to meet Charlotte and Richard. It was being held at my house and I actually preferred it that way as I felt much happier fighting my corner when on my territory. I'd have been much more nervous and intimidated if we were all meeting in an office.

On the morning of the meeting, I tidied the front room and arranged for Pam to take Evie and Elliot out. I knew from experience that potential adopters always arrived early as they're so keen, and Richard and Charlotte were the first to arrive. They must have arranged to meet Karen outside because she was with them.

'It's lovely to meet you,' I told them.

'Likewise,' said Charlotte, shaking my hand.

I liked them instantly. They were both very smiley and I could tell they were genuine smiles and not fake polite ones. They were really warm and friendly and, without hesitation, I knew the moment that they walked through the door that they were the right parents for Evie and Elliot. It was such a relief. I really believe in the adoption process and there's something magical about it when it's a good match and you just know it's going to work. Unfortunately when it doesn't feel right there's not a lot you can do but voice your concerns to the social worker.

'We're very excited to hear more about the children and get things moving,' said Richard.

I could see they wanted these children so badly and were committed to them. In the front room I'd set out twelve albums on the table full of the photos I'd taken of Evie and Elliot since they'd been with me.

'I know you must be desperate to see your children so I thought you could take these albums away with you and have a look in your own time,' I told them.

'That's lovely,' said Charlotte. 'Thank you.'

They were delighted and I could tell they wanted to flick through them straight away.

I made sure that I always referred to them as 'your' children as I knew that it was really important for them to feel a sense of ownership. I knew they'd really register that and think, *Oh she said 'your' children she must really want us to have them.*

I could see that Richard and Charlotte were very nervous and I really felt for them. They wanted these kids so badly and they were so near yet still so far. This house was where their children slept, ate and played. Their things were all around them but they couldn't see them yet and that must have been so frustrating.

We clicked straight away and they were the kind of people I would have been friends with in real life. Charlotte and I dressed alike in tunic tops and leggings and I noticed we had similar tastes in scarves and bags, which I knew would help Evie to settle.

'It sounds strange but you really do look like Evie,' I told Charlotte. 'You're like two peas in a pod.'

She smiled. 'Do you think so?' I could tell that she was really pleased.

I knew they'd be warm and nurturing with the kids, which was exactly what they needed, and I could tell that they had a strong relationship. They were affectionate and loving towards each other and they weren't afraid to show it. I noticed that Richard squeezed Charlotte's hand a few times when she was talking and they looked lovingly at each other.

Andrew introduced everybody and then it was straight down to business.

'We need to get a plan in place about when we introduce Evie and Elliot to Richard and Charlotte and that all depends on when a good time to move them would be. What do you think, Maggie?'

I took a deep breath.

'Well, I believe that we shouldn't rush this as I think the children need more time,' I said.

'In what way?' asked Karen, playing devil's advocate as usual.

I talked about Elliot's lack of attachment and how I didn't think he could transfer that yet, and how unfamiliar situations and adults still made him anxious.

'I don't think enough time and space has passed since he said goodbye to his birth parents and he's still processing that,' I said. 'He could do with a few more months of stability and routine and the chance to be a normal little boy, then I believe he'll be ready.'

I also mentioned the fact that Evie called me Mummy before Karen brought it up.

'I know Karen thinks it's a problem that Evie calls me Mummy, but honestly I'm telling you that it's not a worry. It was just her age and the stage she was at when she first came to live with me. She needed a mummy and I was there to fit the bill.'

I could hear Karen tut-tut-tutting away in the corner.

I knew how much Richard and Charlotte wanted Evie and Elliot and I felt mean trying to delay it but I wanted to explain to them why.

'You're the right parents for these kids and I want you to have them, it's just the wrong time,' I told them. 'Evie and Elliot *will* be yours; however, if the adoption takes place now I truly believe that it will break down because Elliot is not ready. Evie is almost there, but if Elliot isn't accepting of something then she won't be either.'

What I knew would happen is that Elliot would have played up and had endless temper tantrums as he struggled to bond with Richard and Charlotte. I'd got twenty years of experience in dealing with neglected children and coming up with distraction techniques but Richard and Charlotte didn't have that and it wouldn't be fair on them. They'd find it very hard to cope and I just couldn't risk the adoption failing.

'What do you feel you need then, Maggie?' asked Andrew.

'Time,' I said. 'All I'm asking for is a few more months to work on some of the issues the children still have.'

Andrew pointed out that Elliot was due to start primary school in a few weeks.

'That's a huge change for him,' he said. 'Maggie feels that's a lot for him to cope with in itself and it would be too much upheaval for him to start school at the same time as moving to a new family and I tend to agree with her.'

Anna the play therapist then talked about how both Evie and Elliot struggled with the change of venue for their sessions and were highly anxious and withdrawn throughout.

'I don't believe they're ready for adoption yet,' she said. 'It will only unsettle them and add to their stress levels.'

I could see Charlotte and Richard were disappointed.

'You can have my telephone number and my email and I promise you I will keep in touch,' I told them. 'I'll speak to you every day and tell you what your children have been doing and send you photographs of them.'

I knew it was a big ask. The ideal scenario for them would have been to get the children as soon as possible.

'We trust you and we trust your judgment,' said Charlotte. 'You know the kids so we're willing to work with you.'

'We just want the children to be happy and settled and for this to work,' said Richard. 'And if that means waiting a few more months then that's what we'll have to do.'

I was so impressed that they'd accepted what I was saying and they were able to see things from the children's point of view rather than their own, which was a damn sight more than Karen seemed able to do. I felt that she was really annoyed everyone had voted against her. It seemed that she thought we were pandering to the kids and that we just needed to get on with it.

Andrew had been a complete star and had backed me up completely.

'Right, well I think the general agreement seems to be that we delay the adoption and leave Maggie to work with the children for the next few months,' he said. 'That means Elliot can get settled into school and we'll get the excitement of Christmas out of the way and then introduce Richard and Charlotte to Evie and Elliot sometime in the new year.'

It was such a relief and I knew it was the right decision for the kids.

After the meeting I took Richard and Charlotte around the house and showed them Evie and Elliot's bedroom, the kitchen and the playroom. I wanted them to feel comfortable here and to know where their children were living. By the time they left, we were all gassing away like old friends.

'Thank you for listening to my concerns,' I said. 'And I meant what I said about keeping in touch. I'll drop you an email tonight and remember you can give me a ring any time if you want to ask me anything.'

As I waved them off, I felt really happy. I'd got another six months to work with the children without anyone breathing down my neck. They needed that space and time to have a bit of normality and stability in their lives and then I was sure that they would be ready. They *had* to be ready. Whatever happened, there was no way that this adoption could break down. It had to work for Evie and Elliot's sake.

TWENTY-TWO

The Luxury of Time

Elliot strutted around the classroom like a peacock proudly modelling his new jumper.

'This one's just right, Maggie,' he said. 'I love it.'

'I want one too,' moaned Evie. 'I want a school jumper.'

I shook my head.

'I'm sorry, Evie,' I told her. 'It's Elliot who's going to big school not you. You don't need one.'

We were at Elliot's new primary school for a settling-in day before the summer holidays. It was a chance to look around the classrooms and buy his uniform before he started there in September.

I knew starting school was a big step for Elliot and I wasn't sure how he was going to cope with it. It had taken such a long time for him to settle into nursery. But I needn't have worried. As soon as we'd arrived at the school he'd spotted four or five children that he already knew from his nursery. He was delighted to see his little friends and he went running off to play with them.

'Well, Maggie, it looks like you're not going to have a problem there.' Mrs Moody the head teacher smiled.

I'd been sending children to her school ever since I'd started fostering and we had a good relationship. Mrs Moody was wonderful and she was happy to work with me and think outside the box about what my kids needed. She always came up with new and innovative ways to help them. It made life so much easier for me to have someone like that on my side. She'd take foster children even when the paperwork hadn't come through yet as she knew all about the system and how long things took. I owed her a lot and we had a great deal of respect for each other.

I always went to see her when I had a looked-after child joining the school and I'd already had a chat to her about Elliot.

'So what can you tell me about him?' she'd said.

I'd explained how hopefully he was going for adoption in a few months.

'All we really need to focus on is giving him stability and helping to boost his self-esteem,' I'd told her. 'I'm a bit worried about how he's going to settle as he has been very anxious in the past but hopefully he'll be fine.'

Watching Elliot excitedly pick out his new uniform, I felt really positive about him starting school and I could see he felt really grown up and special. Evie, on the other hand, had the most almighty tantrum about not being allowed to buy a school jumper.

'OK, Evie, you can carry the bag if you want,' said Elliot, and thankfully that seemed to appease her.

I was worried that Elliot would be very clingy when we went to see his new classroom but he loved it. He was happy to go off independently and play with the toys with his friends from nursery and I was amazed by how confident he seemed.

'Now you must be Elliot,' said his teacher, Miss Wilson. 'Are you looking forward to coming to big school?'

Elliot went very shy and hid behind my legs. I felt his little hand reach for mine and I gave it a squeeze. Once he'd got that reassurance it gave him the confidence to speak to her.

'Yes, I like big school,' he told her.

I was thrilled with the way he joined in with all the activities without any hesitation. He sang songs with the teacher and did all the actions along with the other children. He wasn't reserved or withdrawn like I had expected; he was delighted.

All through the summer holidays he talked excitedly about school and he couldn't wait to start. On his first day I helped him get ready into his brand new, freshly washed uniform. I combed his hair which had been cut into what my kids cruelly referred to as a pudding basin. I was so proud of him and he had the biggest smile on his face.

'Let me take a photo,' I said, reaching for my camera.

I made a mental note to send a copy to Richard and Charlotte. What struck me as I quickly glanced at the picture was how tiny he looked. Elliot was a petite little thing anyway but his new uniform swamped him and his book bag was nearly half the size of him.

Please let it be OK, I thought, as I led him by the hand into the playground. I really didn't want him to feel anxious or frightened about going to school.

'Bye, Maggie,' he said.

'Have a lovely day,' I told him, giving him a cuddle.

Then he walked off cheerfully into his new classroom without even a backward glance. I smiled to myself as Evie and I waved him off. There hadn't even been a single tear. The only person who wasn't happy was Evie, who remained miffed that she wasn't going to big school like her brother.

Andrew phoned me later that morning.

'Well?' he asked. 'How did he get on?'

'Honestly, Andrew, he was amazing. He trotted in there all happy without any problems at all. He seems to have taken to school like a duck to water.'

It had gone better than any of us could ever have imagined. He came out smiling when I went to pick him up later that afternoon.

'Did you enjoy it?' I said. 'What did you do?'

'Nuffink.' He shrugged.

'Did you have a nice time though?' I asked and he nodded his head.

We came home and had tea and afterwards he and Evie watched some telly. The poor little thing must have been exhausted because when I looked around a couple of minutes later he was flat out, fast asleep on the settee.

As the weeks passed, I could see that going to school had really boosted Elliot's self-esteem and confidence, he'd taken to it so well. I think it was partly because school was seen as a positive thing in our house. He'd watched my kids go happily off to school and he'd helped us bake cakes for Comic Relief and seen them get dressed up for World Book Day, or come home with their special reading books that he always asked to flick through. Now Elliot was doing all these exciting things for himself. He'd even asked to go to a football club after school once a week and had taken great delight in wearing his new football kit and boots.

'Elliot, come and play dollies with me,' Evie asked him one afternoon after school.

Elliot would normally always oblige and allow himself to be bossed around by Evie and be told where the baby needed to go or what she needed to be fed. But this time he shook his head.

'I'm sorry, Evie,' he said very seriously. 'I'm at big school now and I don't play dollies. I play football.'

I smiled to myself but Evie was not impressed.

While all this was going on, I'd kept my promise to Richard and Charlotte about keeping in touch. Every night I emailed them a paragraph or two about the children and what they'd been up to, funny things they'd said or new things they'd done. It was useful as it gave them chance to learn about the kids before they went to live with them. By the time it came to meeting them they'd know everyone in their lives and their likes and dislikes and little habits. It was silly things like telling them Elliot had gone off baked beans or Evie liked her ham sandwiches with the crusts cut off. Someone had bought Tess a chocolate fountain for her birthday and Evie and Elliot loved it when I got it out one weekend. They loved dipping bits of chopped up fruit into it. 'According to Elliot, satsumas dipped in chocolate are the best thing ever,' I wrote. 'But Evie preferred the strawberries.'

I also took daily photos of the kids and sent them to them. They weren't smiley, posed pictures, they were of different faces so they knew the children's expressions and what they meant. I showed them Evie's mardy face and Elliot's expression when he was concentrating. It was like giving them a photo guidebook to the kids, so by the time it came to meeting them they would feel like they would already know everything about them.

It also worked the other way, too. Now I knew things about Richard and Charlotte I could prepare the kids – like the fact they had a dog. I'd make sure that when we went out I'd point out dogs and say, 'Oh I wish we had one of those. Dogs are such lovely pets.' Then when they did meet Charlotte and Richard, the dog would be a real positive.

Whether we were emailing or chatting on the phone, I was developing a real friendship with Charlotte and Richard too. The more I got to know them, the more I liked them and I was so happy that they were going to be the children's new parents. The only hard thing was keeping it to myself. It was so frustrating not being able to share the good news with Evie and Elliot yet. Whenever they asked about when their new mummy and daddy was coming I'd say, 'Don't you worry, Andrew's still looking and hopefully he'll have some news soon.'

The sad fact was nothing was ever definite in the adoption process. Unfortunately I knew from past experience that adoptions break down at every stage. I'd had parents pull out halfway through meeting the kids or even a few weeks after the children had gone to live with them. It was always heartbreaking when that happened but I had to stay positive that this was going to work for Evie and Elliot.

One thing I was keen to get Elliot in particular to do was to be confident and comfortable around unfamiliar adults. By the time it came to moving he'd be comfortable with his adoptive parents but there would be lots of other new people in his life and I wanted him to have a sense that adults were OK.

Every week I gave him and Evie a pound pocket money and he'd put it in his little Fireman Sam purse. Once a week after school I'd take him to the shop and he was allowed to choose some sweets, but the deal was he had to take them up to the counter and give the shopkeeper the money himself.

Friday night in our house was chip shop tea and Elliot loved coming to the fish-and-chip shop with me.

'I'll order them but you have to pay,' I told him.

His eyes lit up when I gave him a £10 note.

'Wow, I'm rich,' he gasped. 'Imagine how much Lego I could buy with this.'

I could tell he was nervous at first giving the woman behind the counter the money, but slowly he got more confident and it became our little routine. Every week he looked forward to coming with me and giving the £10 to the lady to pay for the fish and chips.

I was also keen for both kids to build on their relationship with Karen and Andrew. Karen was never going to be my favourite person, but I knew once Evie and Elliot went to live with Richard and Charlotte it was her and Andrew who they'd be staying in contact with, so it was important that they all had a positive relationship.

'Are there any other sticking points that you think it might be worth us working on with the kids?' Andrew asked.

'Well you know how they reacted when you asked to take them for a walk a couple of months ago,' I said. 'I need to try and get them used to going off with other adults that aren't me.'

They'd been quite resistant in the past to being with other grown-ups. So we arranged for Andrew and Karen to come round one night after school and offer to take the kids out for dinner. They arrived earlier in the day and spent an hour playing with Evie and Elliot.

'Oh, I don't know what to do for tea tonight,' I said. 'I haven't got much in and I'm not that hungry.'

'Well, Maggie, how about I take Evie and Elliot to McDonald's for tea?' Andrew suggested.

Both kids jumped up and started leaping around excitedly.

'Yes, yes, yes!' they chanted.

'I think that's a yes then.' Karen smiled.

They both practically ran out of the door and into Karen's car. It might have been the promise of a burger and fries that convinced them, but no matter what had been on offer, a few months ago I knew neither of them would have gone anywhere without me. But now they were happy to go off.

There were other ways I could see their anxiety had slowly lessened over time. One day I decided to plug the doorbell back in as a bit of an experiment. When it eventually rang, both Elliot and Evie ran to the door ahead of me. They couldn't wait to get there and see who it was, instead of bolting in fear to the other end of the house like they used to do. It turned out to be Simon.

'How are things?' he said.

'Brilliant.' I smiled. 'See for yourself.'

I set another little test for me to show off how far the children had come. When Simon had been there a little while, I got up and grabbed my car keys. 'I'm just popping out to get a bag of sugar,' I said. 'Simon will stay with you.'

Evie carried on playing and Elliot looked up as I walked out of the kitchen but didn't say a word.

'How have they been?' I asked when I came back ten minutes later.

'Not a peep,' said Simon. 'They've been absolutely fine.'

Things that they would have blown a gasket at a few months ago caused them no stress or anxiety now.

These were all important things for Elliot, but I knew the one thing that he needed the most above anything else was time. I was grateful to have been given these extra six months to make sure that he was ready to be adopted. A lot of it wasn't about doing anything in particular with him, it was just about the passing of time and leaving him be. The next few months were all very relaxed and there were no meetings, contact visits, emotional goodbyes or social workers breathing down our necks. Looked-after kids are constantly being poked and prodded and assessed, and it was nice for Elliot to have time and space to be a normal little boy. He needed life to be calm and mundane, boring even. His anxiety had lessened not because of anything special that I had done just because of time, routine and normality. It was nice for my children, too, to get a bit of peace back in our lives.

Before I knew it, we were on the countdown to Christmas. This year Evie and Elliot needed no encouragement. They knew exactly what it was about and they loved the build-up. They were even happy about Santa coming down the chimney, so on Christmas Eve I carefully cut out a template of a big footprint and used talcum powder to make footprints coming from the chimney to the huge piles of presents. As I wheeled Evie's *Dora the Explorer* bike and Elliot's *Spiderman* one into the living room, I felt a tinge of sadness that this would be their last Christmas with us. But there was no use moping, I had to focus on the positive and how pleased I was that they were getting Charlotte and Richard as parents.

Elliot absolutely loved his new bike and, much to my amazement, he was mega confident on it. So much so that just a few days after we got it I took the stabilisers off.

After New Year, it was time to get the kids ready for the first day back at school. I lay the uniforms out the night before all ready for the next morning. I got out Elliot's polo shirt, trousers and pants, and lay them out in his room. As I got a pair of *SpongeBob SquarePants* socks out of his drawer, something suddenly struck me. His whole drawer was full to the brim with literally hundreds of pairs of socks but I couldn't remember the last time Elliot had kicked up a fuss about them or refused to put them on. He still liked colourful socks rather than plain ones, but whatever I put out in the morning he just put straight on without a grumble. I didn't know when socks had stopped being an issue but somehow, without any of us noticing, they just had.

New Year also meant that it would soon be time to introduce Richard and Charlotte to the children. I'd sent them loads of photos of Christmas and the kids on their bikes.

'I hope you don't mind me mentioning this, Maggie,' Charlotte said, when we were chatting on the phone. 'Richard's very safety conscious and he wondered if it would be possible to get the children a helmet each for when they're riding their bikes.'

'Of course,' I said.

Next weekend I took them to the bike shop and bought them a helmet each. While we were there Evie spotted a doll's basket.

'Please can I have this for the front of my bike?' she pleaded.

'And can I have a bell?' begged Elliot.

'I tell you what,' I said. 'I'll buy you them and we'll put them in the cupboard, and when you meet your new daddy we'll get him to put your basket and your new bell on your bikes. Is that a deal?'

Both Evie and Elliot nodded.

It was always good to have an activity or something he could do to bond with the children. Something that Elliot would love and might help Evie be less wary.

'When *will* our new mummy and daddy be coming?' sighed Elliot on the way home from the bike shop.

'Soon, lovey,' I told him. 'Very soon.'

Now I could confidently say that Elliot was as ready as he'd ever be to move on. It was time to introduce Evie and Elliot to their new mummy and daddy.

TWENTY-THREE

Introductions

After months of waiting and preparation, the time had finally come to tell Evie and Elliot the good news.

'I've had a phone call from Andrew and guess what? He's found you a new mummy and daddy,' I told them.

I could see Elliot slowly absorbing what I was saying.

'A new mummy and daddy?' he asked. '*Our* mummy and daddy, just for us ones?'

'Yes, this mummy and daddy are special ones just for you,' I told him. 'The only children they want are you and Evie.'

He gave me a big smile and I could see that he was happy. Evie took her cues from Elliot and once she could see that he was pleased, she joined in with the excitement.

'My new mummy and daddy!' she said, jumping up and down with glee.

'Andrew's got you both a special book each all about them and your new house and he's going to come round with Karen today and give them to you.'

Thankfully both children seemed thrilled about that, and

a couple of hours later Andrew and Karen arrived with the special books. They were a photo album each that Richard and Charlotte had filled with photographs of them and their close family members, and pictures of their house, the garden and the children's new bedrooms.

'This is your new mummy and daddy, Richard and Charlotte,' I said, showing them their photo.

'They look very kind, don't they?' I said. 'They look like a really good mummy and daddy.'

Flicking through them, it was little things the children noticed, like the fact they had a TV on the wall like we did and a trampoline in the garden like ours.

'Look, they've got a dog,' I said, pointing to the photo of a spaniel. 'It says his name is Rufus.'

'I really wanted to live in a house with a dog,' said Elliot, pleased as punch.

I'd had a chat to Charlotte and Richard about the little tricks that always worked well with young children. 'They love having toy ducks in their bath,' I'd said. 'So why don't you get a toy duck and have him in all the photos so it's as if he's showing them around their new house?'

It worked a treat, and the kids smiled when they saw Dan the duck popping up in all the pictures. They both particularly loved the photographs of their new bedrooms. I'd chatted to Charlotte and Richard about what decor the kids would like and Evie's was pink with a lovely white sleigh bed that Charlotte had had as a girl and Elliot's was blue with planets and spaceships on the walls. I'd also helped them decide which photographs to include, like one of the trampoline which I knew they'd love and a picture of two new toothbrushes in the bathroom so I could point them out to them. I knew that showing little things like that would help them feel settled and wanted.

Both Evie and Elliot seemed really pleased and proud of their books and immediately ran to show them to Tess, Pete and Sam.

'Well that went well,' said Karen.

'Yes, they seem really excited,' I replied.

The plan was to give them a few days to look at their books and absorb all the information. Then they'd finally meet Richard and Charlotte and start the two-week settling-in period before they went to live with them permanently. We'd timed it so it would happen in the February half-term holiday when Evie and Elliot wouldn't be at school or nursery.

The children carried their books around with them all day and they even insisted on taking them to bed with them that night. The following day they brought them into school and nursery to show their teachers. I made sure that everyone involved in the children's lives knew what was happening, and Richard and Charlotte had already been to the school and the nursery to talk to the teachers about Evie and Elliot and what they might need going forward when they moved.

Over the next few days we talked about their books continually. When I was making breakfast I said, 'Has your new house got a toaster like ours? Did you see it in the photos of the kitchen?'

Then it would give them an excuse to get out their books and have another look through them. They were keen to show them off to anyone who came round. I arranged for my friends and fellow foster carers Anne, Wendy and Vicky to pop in specially so Evie and Elliot could show them their books and they could be very positive and excited. I asked Simon to drop in too.

'Simon, did you know that Evie and Elliot have had their books about their new mummy and daddy. They're really beautiful. Would you like to have a look at them?

'Elliot, would it be OK if Simon had a look at your book?'

He nodded shyly but he needed no encouragement to open it up and show Simon his new bedroom, Rufus the dog and the trampoline.

Neither of them seemed fearful or anxious about their new home or their new parents. They just seemed happy and excited, and once again that proved to me that they were well and truly ready for adoption.

As usual, Karen was determined to do everything by the book and had the whole first meeting timetabled out.

'We'll do a two-hour introduction on the first day,' she said. 'I'll stay for the first half an hour to check everything's fine.'

'I don't think you can really structure these things,' I told her.

I preferred to play it by ear, see how everyone felt on the day and just go with the flow. I always found the first meeting ended up being longer because the first hour didn't really count as there was always an awkward uncomfortableness that everyone needed to get over before they started relaxing and interacting properly with each other.

Of course children live in the moment and don't have much concept of time, so as usual I didn't tell Evie and Elliot until that morning.

'Guess what?' I said on the first day of the half-term holidays. 'Your new mummy and daddy are coming to see you today.'

I knew from experience that it was good to get the children doing an activity so that when the adoptive parents arrived they could join in with it. It was a great icebreaker and a way of getting everybody comfortable with each other. So I set out some Stickle Bricks on the table and the children started building a tower. They were so involved in their game they didn't even notice when the doorbell rang, so I went to answer it.

'Hello, Richard and Charlotte!' I said loudly.

I made sure that I greeted them with a hug so the children could tell that I was accepting of them.

I could feel their nervous excitement as I led them over to where Evie and Elliot were playing.

'Your new mummy and daddy are here,' I said.

'Hello, kids,' Richard said and Charlotte gave them a nervous smile.

Evie and Elliot just stared at them curiously.

'We were just trying to build a big Stickle Brick mountain,' I told them. 'Do you want to come and help?'

Richard and Charlotte sat down at the table and joined in. As they played, I could see Charlotte watching the children, taking in every little bit of them. Her eyes were all glassy with tears and I knew she was probably thinking, *These are my babies*. These were the children that she'd waited so long for, and now she'd finally met them and I could see it was very emotional for her.

Richard was more practical and he threw himself into helping the kids build the world's biggest tower. I could tell Elliot was impressed and he kept having sneaky glances at his new parents whom he was clearly intrigued by. Evie didn't say much but she was happy joining in with the game.

'Oh no, I can't reach,' said Elliot, desperately trying to put the last brick on the top.

'Shall I lift you up?' asked Richard.

Elliot nodded, so Richard picked him up and Elliot proudly put the final brick on their Stickle Brick creation.

'Well, I think that's the best tower that I've ever seen,' I said.

The first hour was all about Stickle Bricks, and as per her schedule Karen made her excuses and left half an hour into it.

'I'm going to make a cup of tea now so, Elliot, please could you ask your new mummy and daddy if they'd like sugar and milk?'

I made sure I referred to them as your 'new mummy and daddy' rather than 'Charlotte and Richard', in the hope the children would quickly move on to calling them just 'mummy and daddy'. I kept making them ask little questions to try and engage them.

Up until now Evie had been quite reserved and had stood back a little, which wasn't like her. She'd been hovering near Charlotte although she hadn't spoken to her. I think somehow she knew what a momentous moment this was in her life, it was bigger than her, if you like, and she was overwhelmed by it all. The thing Evie loved most in the world was her dolls. She adored her 'babies' as she called them and if she allowed you to touch her babies then it meant you were accepted.

'Evie, why don't you show your new mummy your babies?' I suggested.

'Yes, I'd love to see them,' said Charlotte.

Evie gingerly went over to the settee with her and got out all her dolls. She handed one to Charlotte.

'The baby's crying and she needs a kiss and a bottle,' she told her.

'Shall I kiss her on her head?' asked Charlotte. 'Or on her nose or maybe her ear?'

That made Evie giggle and soon they were engrossed in pretending to feed and change the babies.

Elliot, meanwhile, had spotted that Richard had the biggest bunch of keys that you could possibly imagine sticking out of his pocket. Keys were very important to Elliot and they signified security and safety, and I could tell he was intrigued.

'What do they all open?' he asked and Richard patiently went through every single one with him, telling him exactly what it unlocked.

I just sat at the table and drank my tea watching what was going on. It was important for the children to know that I was still there, but I didn't get involved. I'd occasionally chip in with the odd comment.

'Is that your baby crying, Evie? Do you think she needs some milk?' or 'Elliot, that looks like such a good, strong tower. I bet that will never fall down.'

However, both of them seemed absolutely fine and they weren't looking to me for reassurance. I usually found that first meetings were generally a good reflection of how things were going to go with the adoption, and this one was going brilliantly. Any awkwardness or nervousness soon went and I could see the children were enjoying the individual attention and playing with their new parents.

'Why don't you go and show your new mummy and daddy your bedrooms?' I suggested after a while, when I could see they were getting restless.

They all went upstairs to explore the house that, unbeknown to them, Richard and Charlotte had seen before. I hovered around putting clean towels in the bathroom and tidying Sam and Pete's bedroom. I wanted the kids to know that I was still around but they weren't calling for me or running backwards and forwards to me for reassurance. They were completely absorbed in being with their new parents and that was wonderful.

I couldn't help but listen to what they were saying. I heard Elliot pointing out our collection of rubber ducks in the bathroom and they both showed them their toys. Evie took great delight in talking them through her shoe and handbag collection. Inevitably I knew the tour of the house would end up in the garden where the kids loved to play.

'Make sure you come round willing to bounce,' I'd prewarned Charlotte. 'Because I can guarantee you'll end up in the garden on that trampoline.'

Sure enough, I came out ten minutes later to find them all laughing and jumping up and down on the trampoline. I could see Elliot and Evie thought it was lovely and they looked so happy.

'Well, you all look like you're having fun,' I said, and Charlotte gave me a knowing smile.

I left them to it but Charlotte came to find me in the kitchen.

'Maggie, do you mind if I ring my mum and ask her to pop round and collect our keys?' she said. 'We've been here much longer than we thought we'd be and the dog needs letting out for a wee.'

'Of course,' I said. 'No problem.'

Charlotte was back outside in the garden, so when her mum came to the door, I answered it to give her the keys.

'While you're here would you like to come and meet your new grandchildren?' I said.

Her face lit up.

'Really?' she said. 'I didn't think I'd be allowed.'

'I'm sure it'll be fine to pop your head round and say hello for a few minutes,' I said.

As I took her out to the garden, I could see she was so excited.

'Oh look, Elliot and Evie, it's your grandma,' said Charlotte. 'Do you want to quickly say hello.'

'Hello, Grandma,' they said and carried on bouncing.

It wasn't a big thing for them and she was literally there for a few minutes, but I could see that it had meant the world to her.

When I showed her back out, she had a huge smile on her face.

'Thank you so, so much,' she said. 'I'm so grateful.'

'You're welcome.' I smiled. 'But don't tell anyone otherwise I'll get into trouble.'

She crept out with her finger over her lips.

Adoptive couples are normally advised to isolate themselves for the first few weeks and not see anyone so it's just them and the kids, but personally I don't believe in that. Being alone with two young children can be quite oppressive and boring and I think adults need other adults' company. Plus it's like when you have a new baby. You're so proud of that baby and you can't wait to show it off, and adopting children is no different. I believe there's nothing wrong in having the odd quick visit from close family or friends so you can introduce the kids to the people they're going to have in their lives in a natural and relaxed way. I think sometimes the rules around adoption are a bit too rigid, and parents should be able to do what they think is best.

The first meeting had gone on for much longer than we'd thought and after three hours I could tell everyone was exhausted and it was time to wrap it up.

'Your new mummy and daddy have got to go now,' I told the children. 'But they're coming back to see you again tomorrow.'

We took them out to the hallway and, without any encouragement, Evie gave Charlotte a hug and Elliot hugged both her and Richard. Evie didn't give Richard a cuddle but I didn't want to push her and I wasn't worried. She wasn't fond of men in general and I knew she'd come round to him in her own time. I was pleased and surprised that Elliot was being so affectionate though. I always thought that he would be the one who would be wary of having a mummy but he seemed really relaxed with Charlotte.

'See you tomorrow.' They waved as we watched them get into their car.

Afterwards we talked about them for the rest of the day and it was all massively positive.

'Did you like them?' I asked. 'Did you think they were lovely?' And they both nodded.

'When will we meet the dog?' Elliot asked.

'Later this week you'll be able to go and have a look at your new house and you'll meet Rufus then,' I said.

As soon as Pete, Sam and Tess got in from their holiday play scheme, Evie and Elliot pounced on them.

'We saw our new mummy and daddy today,' Elliot said proudly.

'What were they like?' asked Tess.

'My new mummy had rings on her fingers, a scarf and rings in her ears,' said Evie.

'And my new daddy had a big bunch of keys,' Elliot chipped in.

Now they'd met their new parents their books had taken on extra significance for the children. They knew the people in the photos and they both pointed out Grandma too. I could see they were both completely enchanted with their new mummy and daddy and that was lovely. I couldn't have asked for more.

Charlotte phoned me later that night.

'Well?' I said. 'How do you think it went today?'

'It was wonderful,' she said. 'It was so, so lovely to see the children in the flesh after hearing about them for so long. We're so happy with them, Maggie, and we can't wait to see them again tomorrow.'

She described how amazed she'd been by how eloquent Evie was and how tiny and petite Elliot's hands were, which they hadn't picked up from the photos. I could see that today had been like Christmas for them. They'd heard about these children for so many months and had got to know them but hadn't met them yet. Now they finally had and they were completely and utterly in love with them.

'How do *you* think it went?' Charlotte asked me nervously.

'Honestly, I think it went brilliantly,' I reassured her. 'The children seemed happy and comfortable with you and they're looking forward to seeing you again.'

That night they both insisted on going to sleep with their books.

'Remember you'll see your new mummy and daddy in the morning,' I told them and they both gave me a little smile.

The whole first meeting had gone better than I ever could have expected. I just hoped and prayed the rest of the week was going to be the same.

TWENTY-FOUR

A New Home

The following morning the children couldn't wait to see their new parents again. In fact at breakfast Elliot's first question was, 'What time is my daddy coming round today?'

I was taken aback that he'd already dropped the 'new' and, one day in, they were now just Mummy and Daddy to him. It was wonderful to hear, especially as he was the one that I'd been worried about all along. But whatever Charlotte and Richard had, it had met Elliot's needs and he saw them as his parents.

I'd arranged for them to come round for lunch, and the kids helped me prepare the food. We chopped up some carrots and cucumber and Evie managed to turn some hard-boiled eggs into a crumbly mess.

Both of them asked Richard and Charlotte lots of questions.

'Do you like salad?' Elliot asked.

'Do you like eggs?' said Evie. 'I like eggs.'

'What colour are your slippers?' Elliot asked Charlotte and we all laughed.

None of us had any idea where that random question had come from.

'They're pink fluffy ones,' Charlotte told him.

'Oh why can't I have pink fluffy slippers?' sighed Evie.

'You've got your lovely pink *Peppa Pig* slippers, haven't you?' I reminded her.

It was like having old friends round for lunch and everyone was happy and relaxed. Nothing had to be staged and it all felt very natural. It was pouring down with rain so playing in the garden was out and everything was more chilled out and less frantic than the day before. Richard and Charlotte did some puzzles with the kids and we talked about what they wanted to do the following day.

'I'd like to go for a ride on my new bike,' said Elliot.

Evie went off and started rummaging round in the cupboard and I wondered what she was doing until she dragged out the doll's basket we'd bought for her bike and Elliot's new bell.

'Well remembered,' I told her. 'I did say your new daddy would be able to put those on your bikes for you.'

We all looked expectantly at poor Richard and he promised that he'd bring his tools round the following day. I could see Elliot was very impressed by that.

'My daddy's going to put my bell on my bike,' he said proudly.

'And my daddy's going to put my doll basket on,' said Evie, copying her brother.

Evie was still very wary of Richard, but I wasn't overly worried as I knew it was nothing to do with the adoption and more to do with her wariness of the whole male population. In fact, Charlotte and I giggled about her complete dismissal of him even though he was trying so hard with her.

'Shall I help you to feed your babies?' he asked, picking up one of her dolls. 'I think she'd like a bottle.'

But Evie just gave him a withering look.

'No, thank you,' she said. 'New Mummy do it.'

I was still 'Mummy' and Charlotte was 'New Mummy'. It didn't seem to worry Charlotte in the slightest and we all talked about it openly.

'What's my name?' I asked Evie.

'Mummy,' she replied.

'No, I mean my real name that everyone else calls me by.'

'Maggie,' she said.

'That's right,' I told her. 'Do you think you could call me Maggie?'

But she just gave me a sly smile.

The children had accumulated so much stuff since they'd come to live with me that I wanted to start gradually moving it over to Charlotte and Richard's. Also I thought it was important that when Evie and Elliot went to their look around their new house later in the week there would already be some of their things in the drawers and out on display. I knew it would be nice and comforting for them to see their belongings around the house even though they'd never lived there, and it would help them feel more settled. That morning Richard and Charlotte had brought two big storage boxes with them. Although I was going to sort through most of their stuff and pack it myself, I wanted Elliot and Evie to feel in control and decide what went first.

'Right, kids, because you've got so many things and it won't all fit in the car we need to start sending stuff to your new house,' I said. 'So you need to choose some things to send back with Charlotte and Richard and put them in your box.'

I knew it was very important to reassure Elliot about this as one of his big fears was that his things weren't going to go with him and he would be left with nothing like when he first arrived at my house.

'You're in charge,' I told him. 'So over the next few days you need to go round and find all your things because everything is going with you.'

Elliot filled his box with action men and dinosaurs, while Evie put in a tiara, a few of her handbags and some stuffed toys that she never really played with.

'Don't worry, you don't have to take your very favourite things until the last day,' I reassured them.

The time just flew by and, before we knew it, Richard and Charlotte had been with us for most of the day. According to Karen's timetable they weren't supposed to give the kids a bath until much later in the week, but Evie and Elliot seemed keen for them to stay so we took our cues from them. The idea was that during the settling-in period they did bath times and bedtimes and even came round early one morning so they learned their morning routine, but they already knew most of it from chatting to me over the past few months. They gave them a bath while I just sat on the floor and watched.

'Elliot likes his bath nice and warm, don't you?' I said. 'And they both love their collection of rubber ducks so we'll have to make sure you take those with you to your new house.'

The following day Richard kept his promise and fastened Evie's doll basket to her bike and put Elliot's bell on.

'Why don't you take them for a test run to the park?' I said.

This would be a good marker of how they were getting on, as it would be the first time that the children had left the house on their own with Richard and Charlotte. I hoped that they would go with them willingly but if they wouldn't we'd already agreed that I'd go with them to avoid any stress or upset. But thankfully it wasn't a problem. The children went without any hesitation and never even asked if I was coming too.

'Have fun.' I smiled, waving them off. As I closed the front door, I could hear Elliot ringing his new bell all the way up the street.

I knew they'd be tired when they came back so I'd organised a little surprise for them.

'Ladies and gentlemen, welcome to your movie and duvet afternoon,' I said in a grand voice.

I led them into the front room and got them all to sit on the big settee together so they could see the TV. Elliot plonked himself next to Richard and once Evie had organised her dolls on the settee under a blanket, she sat down in between Elliot and Charlotte. Tess and I put duvets over them and then put aprons on and pretended to be waitresses, which Evie and Elliot thought was hilarious.

'Can I take your order, madam?' said Tess to Evie and she wrote all the orders down on a little notebook just like a proper waitress.

We served them drinks and popcorn while they watched the film *Cloudy with a Chance of Meatballs*.

Doing something like this was important as it was a way of getting them used to physical contact. Being huddled up on the settee together gave them a chance to get close to one another and become familiar with each other's bodies and smells. It was a way of them getting used to being in each other's personal space and they could be as cuddly or as uncuddly as they wanted. This was hugely important for Elliot, as he'd had such issues in the past with physical contact, so I was pleased to see that Richard had his arm around Elliot's shoulder and Elliot was leaning into him and looked completely relaxed. Evie was lolled all over Charlotte. She was a real fiddler so she was constantly twiddling with Charlotte's earrings and rings or playing with her scarf.

This was also a really important thing for Richard and Charlotte to do too. They weren't really that interested in the film, I'm sure, but what it did do was give them a chance to study their children – to look at their faces, to get to know them and observe them. Up until now they'd been busy doing activities with them and they'd been on the go constantly. This gave them peace and quiet and a chance to notice their little physical quirks like the birthmark on Evie's neck or Elliot's little scar on his hand where he'd cut himself. It gave them the time to study the children's expressions and to notice what bits of the film made them laugh or feel sad.

Over the next few days Richard and Charlotte took over more of the children's routine. They came round late one afternoon and had dinner with us and this time they gave the children a bath, got them into their pyjamas and tucked them into bed. I was always hovering in the background just for reassurance but it all happened very naturally and Evie and Elliot seemed fine with it.

Once the kids were in bed, Charlotte and Richard stayed around and we all sat in the front room and chatted. They talked through the past few days and asked me lots more questions.

'What can we do to make sure things go smoothly?' said Charlotte.

'I honestly don't think you can do any more,' I told her. 'I think this is the easiest transfer I've ever had to do in my whole career. The children seem happy and they're already really attached to you. Just relax and enjoy it.'

What was nice for me was seeing how in love they were with the kids. They'd had an instant connection with Evie and Elliot and it just reinforced to me what a good match this was. One reason I thought it was going so smoothly was because we were all familiar with each other and they'd had that time to learn all about the kids before meeting them. They already knew their routines and habits and the little things like what Elliot's favourite puzzle was and the song that always made Evie giggle.

'Karen's going to have a fit when she finds out how long you've stayed.' I smiled.

'Do you get on well with her?' Charlotte asked.

I knew I had to be diplomatic with my answer.

'Sometimes in this job you work with people who just aren't your cup of tea,' I said.

'It's funny,' said Charlotte. 'The impression we got from Karen was that you were going to be really difficult to work with but we haven't found that at all.'

I just laughed. 'I don't think I'm Karen's cup of tea either.'

Although I'd developed a friendship with Richard and Charlotte, I had to make sure that I was supervising the hand-over as a professional too. My job as a foster carer was to act in the best interests of the children. I needed to make sure that I was watching out for any anxieties and check their responses to things and judge whether they were normal. I didn't want to miss significant things because I was so comfortable with Charlotte and Richard. But as far as I could see there were no problems and I didn't have any concerns. The kids were completely at ease with it all.

I could see the friendship I'd got with Charlotte and Richard had really helped Elliot to bond with them. He watched us as we laughed and chatted and because we'd got that familiarity and he could tell that I liked them, it almost gave him permission to let go of me and transfer his attachment to them.

Evie was slowly letting go too. I was sitting on the settee with Charlotte one day when Evie came and climbed all over us. Charlotte was wearing a long scarf and Evie unravelled it and wound it round my neck too so that Charlotte and I were bound together.

'Look, Elliot,' she shouted, 'two mummies!'

I thought it was a lovely thing to say, and Charlotte and I laughed. After that it was as if I could see Evie mentally shifting her attachment.

The next morning I went into their bedroom just as Evie was waking up.

'Morning, Maggie,' she said chirpily. 'What time is Mummy coming today?'

And just like that I was back to being Maggie. I must admit it took me by surprise and I had a lump in my throat. For someone who had never been called Mummy before, or even wanted to be, I suddenly felt like I'd lost something. I'd certainly been put in my place but it was a huge statement from Evie. From then on, I was just plain old Maggie while Charlotte, to her delight, was now Mummy.

After five days, we had a planning meeting at my house to discuss how things were going. Karen had her tick list with her and she looked horrified as I told everyone how we were much further ahead than we thought we'd be at this stage.

'So you didn't follow the plan?' she said.

'We went with the children,' I told her. 'There's been absolutely no upset from them at all, so we just went with it and they have been absolutely fine.'

'As far as we're concerned, it couldn't have gone better and Maggie has been brilliant,' said Charlotte.

Andrew had popped in one day and he was impressed by how the children were coping.

'I'm genuinely amazed at the connection that Richard and Charlotte have with the kids,' he said. 'They already look like a family. It's a good job done by all.'

It was going so well that everyone decided that the settling-in period would be shortened to nine days instead of fourteen.

'There's no reason if things carry on like they are why the children can't be with you permanently by Wednesday of next week,' said Andrew.

Charlotte and Richard looked ecstatic.

'We just can't wait to get on with it,' said Richard.

The next day it was time for the children to visit their new house and they couldn't wait, as they'd been looking at photos of it for so long. Both of them had a little decorative suitcase in their room that they kept their most precious things in. Elliot's had his best Lego in it and in Evie's was a little Upsy Daisy and some pens and pencils and little figures. On the morning of the visit I handed them both their suitcases.

'Take these with you to your new house,' I told them. 'Then I want you to find a really special place for them in your new bedrooms and leave them there.'

It was a little mission for each of them.

When Richard and Charlotte dropped them back that night, they were happy bunnies. They loved the dog and their new bedrooms had been a massive hit.

'Please, Maggie, can we sleep there?' asked Elliot.

'Not just yet,' I said.

With little ones I tended to measure things in terms of sleeps.

'Two more sleeps and you're going to go and stay at your new house with Mummy and Daddy for the night. Then you're going to come back here and pack up the rest of your things and you'll have one more night here to say bye-bye and then you'll go to your new house for ever.'

Evie had been particularly taken with her wooden bed and Elliot loved the spaceships on the wall.

'And do you know what, Maggie?' he whispered to me. 'Our new mummy and daddy sleep in the same bed.'

He'd never come across that before and he thought it was funny.

'No way,' I said, playing along with him. 'The poor things have to share. It must be a big bed then?'

'Yes, massive.' He nodded.

The aim of the last few days was to settle them into their new home. The next day they spent the day there with Richard and Charlotte. They had their tea there and a bath, and they dropped them home in their pyjamas.

'We made some buns for everyone,' said Evie, getting out a big box of fairy cakes.

The next day the children went to stay overnight for the first time. Charlotte rang me later and she was all squeaky and excited as she told me how the kids had gone to bed without any problems and were fast asleep.

'You've got your babies at your house now,' I said. 'Do you finally believe that it's going to happen?'

'I know.' She sighed. 'I still can't quite believe it to be honest.'

Charlotte and Richard dropped them off at lunchtime the next day so we could have one last afternoon and evening with Evie and Elliot and say goodbye. The kids were buzzing with excitement.

'Mummy and Daddy took us to buy some new pyjamas, Maggie,' Elliot told me.

'I chose *Peppa Pig* ones so they match my slippers and Elliot's are *Power Rangers*,' said Evie. 'I've left them at my new house as my new bedroom's so big and I don't want to lose them.'

'Well I think you've made two children very happy indeed,' I told Charlotte and Richard.

Tomorrow was going to be a huge day in theirs and Elliot and Evie's lives.

'One more sleep and then they're yours for ever,' I told Charlotte as she left and she squeezed my hand.

'I can't wait,' she said.

It was the start of a new chapter for them but the closing of one for us. As I shut the door, I knew it was time for us to start saying goodbye.

TWENTY-FIVE

Letting Go

Sausage rolls, sandwiches, quiche and fruit kebabs covered the kitchen table. All that needed to be done was to tip some crisps into a bowl and do a jug of orange squash and then I'd finally be ready for the guests to arrive.

It was Evie and Elliot's last night with us and we were having a little party. I didn't want a big, over-the-top affair but I'd arranged for our friends Anne and Vicky to pop in with their kids and say goodbye before they left in the morning. I'd decided to do a buffet tea so everyone could help themselves.

As I was running around the kitchen putting the finishing touches to the spread, my mobile rang. It was Simon.

'Are you ringing to check up on Evie and Elliot?' I said. 'It's going brilliantly and we're having a little get-together tonight before they leave in the morning.'

'That's great,' he replied. 'But actually I was ringing about something else.'

He paused.

'Maggie, a new placement's coming in tomorrow that I thought you might be interested in.'

'Tomorrow?' I said.

'No rest for the wicked,' Simon joked. 'But seriously, Maggie, it's a tricky case and Social Services need an experienced carer like yourself. You know how they value your expertise.'

'Go on then,' I said. 'Stop sweet-talking me and tell me what you know.'

It was a ten-year-old boy called Dan. Simon explained that he'd been in care as his own parents had not been able to look after him and at the age of six he'd been adopted by two teachers. The placement had now fallen apart in very tricky circumstances.

'Poor little lad,' I said, horrified.

How awful to have been given the second chance of a family after years in care and then to be so badly let down by your adopters. It didn't bear thinking about.

'It's all got to be carefully handled,' said Simon.

'Of course we'll take him,' I said, without hesitation.

It was going to be hectic with Evie and Elliot leaving in the morning but I thought it would be good for me to have a fresh challenge and a new focus.

'That's brilliant,' said Simon. 'He's with an emergency foster carer at the minute but his social worker will bring him round tomorrow afternoon as it's crucial we get him settled some-where quickly. Thanks, Maggie.'

'No problem,' I said. 'You know how I like a challenge.'

My mind was buzzing with so many things but I knew I had to focus on saying goodbye to Evie and Elliot. I was determined to keep everything happy and positive as I didn't think it would be beneficial for the kids to have a big, teary goodbye.

'Anne, Wendy and Vicky are going to pop round later to say bye-bye as they might not see you for a little while,' I told them.

They seemed really excited about seeing my friends' kids. They'd brought them good luck cards and little pressies which Evie and Elliot loved.

'Look,' said Evie. 'A teddy bear.'

They'd also got a photo in a frame of them and Anne's children.

The other kids asked Evie and Elliot lots of questions about their new mummy and daddy. Then they went off playing hide and seek around the house leaving me, Anne, Wendy and Vicky to chat.

'They seem so happy and relaxed about it all,' said Wendy.

'That's the first time that I've ever heard Evie calling you Maggie,' said Anne.

It was nice to talk to people who hadn't been involved in the settling-in process and it enabled me to see how much the kids had achieved and grown in the past ten days.

'How are you feeling about it all?' asked Vicky.

'I'm determined not to feel sad,' I said. 'I'm so happy for all four of them and I don't really see it as a goodbye because I know that we're going to see the kids again.'

I told them about the heart-to-heart I'd had with Charlotte when they'd dropped the kids off the night before. I could see they were so excited that Evie and Elliot were finally coming to live with them, but the nerves had started to kick in.

'Do you think this is going to work, Maggie?' Charlotte had asked me, and I'd just laughed.

'Of course it's going to work. Can't you see how well it's all gone?'

'I can, but at the same time part of me is scared,' she'd said.

'It's normal as a parent not to feel in control sometimes, but you and the kids, it was definitely meant to be,' I'd told her.

'Will you always be there for us?' Charlotte had asked me and I'd smiled.

'Absolutely,' I'd said without hesitation. 'I'll be here for you as much as you want me to be. There's only one difference – you have to be the ones who make contact with me, otherwise I'll feel like I'm interfering.'

Even though I'd become friends with her and Richard, I still had to be professional about it. I didn't want them to feel obliged to keep in touch with me once they had the children.

'Well, we're very sure that we want to stay in touch,' Richard had told me.

Neither of them felt that it would cause any problems for them or the kids.

'Well, it's a time issue,' I'd said. 'You have to see what will work for Evie and Elliot.'

I had to think about Sam, Pete and Tess, too. While they'd seen kids come and go before, they were very attached to Evie and Elliot and they'd become part of our family. I knew they were going to miss them terribly, so it was good to be able to reassure them that we'd keep in touch and we were going to see the children again soon. It helped that they liked Richard and Charlotte too and got on well with them.

When we'd had the planning meeting during the settling-in period it had already been decided that the kids and I would go over to Richard and Charlotte's for tea three weeks after they'd left.

As for me, it was always hard when children left, especially ones like Evie and Elliot who I would have willingly kept long term. But part of my job was being able to let go. I'd taught myself to box each child away to a certain extent once they'd gone. Otherwise it didn't enable you to move forward and I'd end up carrying all sorts of emotional baggage around with me.

That night when all our guests had gone home and I'd tidied up, I tucked Evie and Elliot up in bed for the last time.

'One more sleep,' sighed Elliot.

'That's right,' I said. 'Tomorrow you're going to go and live with your new mummy and daddy for ever. Won't that be exciting?'

They both gave me a big grin.

The next morning I woke up to find that Evie had crawled into bed with me.

'What are you doing in my bed?' I smiled.

'I just came to say good morning,' she said.

She hadn't done that for months and I think it was her way of saying goodbye and having a last little moment with me on her own.

The rest of the morning was a mad rush as Richard and Charlotte were coming to collect the children at 9.30 a.m. I helped them get their last few bits together. There were their pyjamas and the clothes they'd had on the day before and Elliot's stuffed toy dog and Evie's two favourite dolls. I put them all in a bag along with their duvet covers that I took straight off their beds without washing them so they'd smell familiar.

It's little things like that that help children to settle. Charlotte and I had already had a chat about the type of washing powder

I used as she wanted to use the same one so the children's clothes smelt similar.

Once I'd packed up their last few things I got them to say goodbye to their bedroom so it would give them a sense of completion.

'Bye-bye room,' they said.

'Now we might be saying goodbye but remember we're going to be seeing you in a few weeks,' I told them. 'We're all coming round for dinner and you can show me your dog and your new bedrooms.'

Evie and Elliot nodded and smiled.

When Charlotte and Richard arrived they ran to the door to greet them. I could see Elliot whispering to Richard and suddenly he brought out a bag.

'Look what we've done for you, Maggie,' said Elliot, handing me a parcel.

'It's a present so you can remember us,' said Evie.

Inside were three wooden heart-shaped photo frames that had pictures of Evie and Elliot in them.

'They're gorgeous,' I said, tears welling up in my eyes. 'Thank you.'

Charlotte had brought me a lovely bunch of flowers.

'These are for you to say thank you for everything,' she said. 'Are you all right?' she asked, stroking my arm.

'I'm absolutely fine,' I said. 'Are you all right?'

But I could see she was on the verge of crying.

'I'm finally going to take my children home,' she said. 'I really can't believe it, Maggie.'

She was very emotional but I knew how much this meant to her and how much she'd wanted a family for so long.

I'd learnt the art of a good goodbye was making it quick, and I didn't want it to drag out. Pam had come round to wave the kids off and everyone was lingering in the hallway.

'Right,' I said, clapping my hands. 'Who needs a wee for the journey?'

Evie and Elliot went to the loo while I gave Charlotte and Richard their bag.

'Thank you,' said Charlotte, giving me a hug. 'Thank you so, so much for everything.'

'Give me a ring later if you want to,' I said.

Then it was time to say goodbye to Evie and Elliot. Sam, Pete and Tess gave them a big hug, and Pam, then finally it was my turn.

'See you very soon,' I told them, giving them a kiss and a cuddle. 'You're so lucky to have such a lovely mummy and daddy.'

We watched them all get into the car. Richard and Charlotte strapped them into their new car seats and wound down the windows.

'Bye-bye and see you very soon,' I shouted.

We all blew kisses and the kids caught them and we smiled and waved as they drove away. As we walked back into the house, I noticed that tears were rolling down Pam's face.

'Well, you can stop that crying for a start because we've got beds to change,' I said, squeezing her hand.

Even though I was going to miss them, I was genuinely excited for them. It had all gone so well and I knew they were going to be happy with Charlotte and Richard. I'd been allowed the privilege of having Evie and Elliot for an extra few months and that decision had paid off. I had the satisfaction of knowing that it was a job well done.

Before I put my new photos up in the front room, I sat down for a moment and looked at them. Evie and Elliot's little faces grinned at the camera as they posed in their new bedrooms. They were smiling and these were proper, genuine smiles that showed in their eyes and made them sparkle. So, so different to the two gaunt, terrified, little children who had arrived on my doorstep nineteen months ago. This was a happy ending and sadly in my job you didn't get too many of those. Some children leave you and you know that's probably the last time that you're ever going to see them again. But I just knew that Evie and Elliot would always be part of our lives and our family.

The next few hours were a race against time to get everything ready for the new placement. I was looking forward to a new challenge and the kids were excited about someone new coming to live with us too. It was hectic but good in a way as there was no time for any of us to mope or feel sad. If the house had been empty for a while then it would have given me time to dwell on things.

Simon called half an hour after Evie and Elliot left.

'How did it go?' he asked.

'It was fine,' I said. 'They were all so excited.'

'Great,' he said. 'And just to let you know your new placement should be with you just after lunch.'

I'd already arranged for a decorator to come to paint the bedroom after Evie and Elliot had gone. I always did this after a long-term placement ended as I think it helped us all to move on – it wouldn't be fair on the new child if we all still referred to it as 'Evie and Elliot's room'. Pam and I dismantled the two toddler beds and erected a single one and we put up new curtains. The decorator arrived and painted a quick coat of blue over the cream walls. Just three hours after Evie and Elliot had left, the room had a completely different feel to it. I think that was important for all of us.

Just before 1 p.m., I was pulling a football duvet on the bed when the doorbell rang.

'Come on, kids,' I shouted. 'That will be the social worker with Dan.'

And as we all hurried to the door to welcome our new placement, I knew a new challenge was just beginning.

Epilogue

There are four photographs that still take pride of place in my front room. The three pictures in the heart-shaped wooden frames that Evie and Elliot gave me before they left and one I've put up since. It's the photo I took of the children on their first walk out of the house and they're pushing their toy prams through the autumn leaves to the postbox. When I see their anxious little faces staring back at me, it makes me appreciate how far they've come in their lives. That photo symbolises the beginning for me. Everything before that picture had been about fear but that walk to the postbox gave me hope and proved to me that things could and were changing.

For the first three weeks after they were adopted, although I didn't see Evie and Elliot, Charlotte phoned me every night to let me know how they were getting on. It was all going really well and the kids had settled in to their new school and nursery.

My children missed Evie and Elliot terribly, and they couldn't wait to go round to their new house for tea. The kids ran to the door when we arrived and greeted us like old friends. They weren't upset or distressed to see us, and they looked like they'd lived there for ever. They were very proud and possessive of their new house and there was a lot of 'this is my' and 'this is our' and they were desperate for us all to see their new bedrooms and admire them.

What really touched me was the care Richard and Charlotte had taken to include our family in Evie and Elliot's new lives. In their bedrooms both children had framed photos of Tess, Pete and Sam, and Charlotte had made spaghetti bolognaise for tea.

We laughed about the fact that Evie still wasn't having much to do with Richard and she'd had a few almighty strops which they'd quickly dealt with. During the settling-in period she'd been an absolute angel but I'd warned Richard and Charlotte what might be to come.

'Blimey, you were right about those.' Charlotte smiled.

Both of them said they were glad that I'd told them the truth about the kids and given them the best and the worst. Then when the worst came they knew how to deal with it and move on.

A couple of weeks after we'd been round there for tea, Charlotte called me.

'We're going to be in the area tomorrow,' she said. 'Can we pop in for a cuppa?'

'Of course you can,' I said.

It was the first time Evie and Elliot had been back to the house but they fitted right in like they'd never been away and my kids were pleased to see them. They were intrigued to meet the new placement Dan.

'Do you want to come and see my bedroom?' he asked them.

'We used to live here, you know,' said Elliot as he swaggered upstairs.

A few weeks later it was Charlotte's birthday and Richard asked if the kids could come for a sleepover while they had a night out. The kids were delighted and to be honest I was honoured. I knew by then that our friendship was going to carry on which was lovely. It's rare to have such regular contact with foster children because some adopters see foster carers as a threat and they want to forget that part of the kids' lives, but Richard and Charlotte have never felt that way. Evie decided she wanted to sleep in Tess's room and Elliot went in with Pete. It all felt really normal and natural and we loved having them.

Evie and Elliot are eleven and twelve now and they're lovely, happy kids. Elliot's past still affected him for a while and he struggled to make genuine friends and was easily led astray. But now he has one or two good mates whom he's close to. He'll always be a quiet, deep thinker while Evie is a happy, bubbly girl who has lots of friends. They're both doing well at school.

Their early childhoods will always have an effect on them but Richard and Charlotte have given them the love and resilience to be able to cope with it and they don't see themselves as different to anyone else. We still see them at least every couple of months and they just fit right back in like they've never been away. Richard and Charlotte have become part of our extended family. They know all my friends like Wendy, Anne and Bob, and Vicky, and if I'm having a party I'll invite them all over. Although their memories have faded now, Evie and Elliot know they used to live with me and they still have a brilliant relationship with Sam, Tess and Pete.

I'm so, so proud of who they've become and so grateful to Richard and Charlotte for giving them a chance to be part of a loving family. It could have been a whole different story if we hadn't fought the fact that they'd been deemed unadoptable so early on. In the end, it was one of the easiest adoptions that I've ever done. Evie and Elliot's story just echoes my belief that there's a family out there for every child no matter how damaged and traumatised they are. It just takes time, love and patience in order to find them.

Acknowledgements

Thank you to my children, Tess, Pete and Sam, who are such a big part of my fostering. To my wide circle of fostering friends – you know who you are! Your support and your laughter is valued. To my long-suffering link worker who always puts up with my moans and groans, Andrew B for your encouragement and care, and to Heather Bishop who spent many hours listening and enabled this story to be told. Thanks also to my literary agent Rowan Lawton and Anna Valentine from Orion for giving me the opportunity to share my stories.

To contact
Maggie Hartley:

EMAIL
maggie.hartley@orionbooks.co.uk

OR GO TO
facebook.com/maggiehartleyauthor

Also by
MAGGIE HARTLEY

Out now in eBook

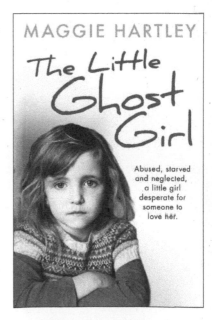

Out now in eBook